dealing
WITH TODAY'S TEENS
A SEMINAR FOR PARENTS AND YOUTH WORKERS

Participant Workbook
With Daily Lessons

COPYRIGHT NOTICE

Reproduction or duplication in any form of any portion of the material contained in this publication is strictly prohibited by US and International copyright law. © Copyright 2008 Heartlight Ministries Foundation. May not be copied without permission from the publisher. All rights reserved.

A publication by Mark Gregston

A production of the
HEARTLIGHT MINISTRIES FOUNDATION
Post Office Box 480 Hallsville, TX 75650
WWW.HEARTLIGHTRESOURCES.ORG
Reorder Line: 866-700-3264

Video Series Credits: Workbook Credits:

Director   *Writer*
David Bolthouse   Tamara Bolthouse

Producer/Writer   *Editor*
Tamara Bolthouse   David Bolthouse

Sound/Camera/Editing/Graphics   *Cover Design*
Jeff Sieh   Blue Star Design

2ⁿᵈ Camera   *Typesetting/Pages Design*
Ben Weinert   Soundview Design Studio

Scripture taken from the HOLY BIBLE, NEW INTERNATIONAL VERSION®. Copyright © 1973, 1978, 1984 International Bible Society. Used by permission of Zondervan. All rights reserved. The "NIV" and "New International Version" trademarks are registered in the United States Patent and Trademark Office by International Bible Society. Use of either trademark requires the permission of International Bible Society.

©Copyright 2008 Heartlight Ministries Foundation. May not be copied without permission from the publisher. All rights reserved.

Contents

Participant Instructions

This workbook an important part of the 8-lesson *Dealing With Today's Teens* video study. Using it will help you remember and apply the video lessons. The daily homework questions will help facilitate discussion within your group the following week and make the study much more thought-provoking.

Be sure to take notes during the video lecture on the pages provided at the beginning of each lesson. Then, work through the daily lesson material by writing down your answers in the spaces provided.

In your group, your facilitator will set aside 40 minutes for discussion and 20 minutes for viewing the teaching. Feel free to carry over to the following week if you need more time to complete one lesson before moving on to the next.

If you missed either of the first two lessons, you may view them online (with a high speed internet connection). The web address is: **http://www.dealingwithtodysteens.org/video.html**.

May God bless you in your study.

Mark Gregston
Teacher

Important Notifications

If you are experiencing difficulties with your teenager that are life-threatening in nature, we encourage you to seek immediate professional help, even as you go through this course. Do not wait. For help in finding a counselor or program to assist your teen, we welcome you to call our national toll-free helpline at **866-700-FAMILY** (3264).

This program is not intended to offer psychological advice or to take the place of professional therapy, counseling or medical treatment. Children currently under the supervision of a professional should not discontinue such care without the consent of this professional. Never discontinue a child's medication without consulting a qualified professional.

All the statements in the *Dealing With Today's Teens* study and this workbook represent the opinions of author, Mark Gregston.

About Your Teacher

Mark Gregston began his work with teens 34 years ago as a youth minister. During the 80's, while acting as Area Director for *Young Life* and living at Kanakuk Kamps in Branson, Missouri, a system of effectively turning around struggling teens began to take shape as they opened their home to teens in crisis.

In 1989, Mark and Jan formalized a therapeutic program for teens and founded *Heartlight*, a residential counseling center for struggling teens located on 100 beautiful acres in the Piney Woods region of East Texas, about 150 miles east of Dallas. *Heartlight* is dedicated to providing counseling and mentoring to bring about needed behavioral changes for 50 troubled teenagers at a time.

For over 20 years, *Heartlight (www.heartlightministries.org)* has helped thousands of families work through difficult situations with their teenagers, and continues to help teenagers develop more positive motivations in life than they once had.

In recent years, Mark and Jan have begun teaching this system to parents nationwide via the radio, the Internet, in church seminars, through books, retreats, and speaking engagements.

Mark and Jan are proud parents and grandparents. Their son Adam lives in Dallas. Their daughter Melissa and her husband Blake Nelson serve as Directors for Heartlight. They live next to the Heartlight campus with their dogs and horses and call Longview, Texas their home.

Understanding Your Teen's Needs

Pre-Evaluation
A tool to help you think about the current status of your teenager.

It is important to take an initial review of where things currently stand with your teenager. If you are not the parent of a teenager, then you may skip this step.

Please mark the severity of the behavior traits below that you are seeing in your teenager.
(0 = Almost Never 1 = Sometimes 2 = Frequently 3 = Very Often)

____Putting self or others in danger
____Selfishness
____Running away
____Swearing/profanity
____Angry outbursts
____Illegal drug use
____Prescription drug abuse
____Tobacco use
____Alcohol use
____Promiscuity
____Eating disorders (over or under eating)
____Sleep disorders (over or under sleeping)
____Anxiety
____Depression/sadness
____Blaming others
____Dark moods
____Suicidal statements
____Addicted to pornography
____Screaming/yelling
____Violent acts or thoughts
____Scared/paranoid
____Vengeful
____Illegal acts
____Meanness/rudeness

____Cutting oneself
____Excessive body piercing
____Homosexual tendencies
____Extreme thrill seeking
____Thievery
____Dishonesty/lying
____Cheating
____School grades suffering
____Loner/despondent
____Truancy
____Avoids family and former friends
____Hatred toward religion
____Sneaks out at night
____Refuses medication
____Seems to be hiding something
____Severe mood swings
____Disrespect for authority
____Meanness to animals
____Severe sibling rivalry
____Extremely demanding
____Disrespectful of personal boundaries
____Addicted to computer games

_____SCORE

If the score is over 30 points, or if your child exhibits suicidal or violent tendencies or drug abuse, he or she may need more serious interventions now. Be sure to contact a qualified professional. Do not wait. Call our toll-free 24-hour Helpline for more help at 866-700-3264.

My Lesson Notes
Understanding Your Teen's Needs

(Fill in the blanks as underlined items show up on the video screen)

Kids are not as _____ as they used to be.

Kids today show parents less _____ and feel more _____.

Today, we _____, _____, and provide for our kids.

We need to _____ them.

We need to _____ our kids.

Kids are not _____ today because we allow them to remain

_____.

We have moved from parenting to _____.

_____ is the #1 thing lacking in homes, schools and work.

Our job as parents is _____ to make sure our children are _____ all
the time, nor is it to make sure that they _____ us.

Children need both: _____ and strong _____ _____.

Significance is not as important to a teen as is _____.

Security is knowing that they _____ have to change to be _____.

Tell them often:
> *"There is nothing you can do to make me _____ more,*
> *and there is nothing you can do to make me _____ less.*

To build a relationship…It is important to _____ _____ together weekly.

To build a relationship…Look for opportunities for _____.

Be quick to _____, slow to _____ and slow to _____.

To build a relationship…Develop a _____ ___ _____.

Help them do more of what they _____ ___ _____ and do it _____.

To build a relationship…Remember the thumbprint of God.

When a child is vile toward you, remember that the _____ _____ _____ is still on their life.

Your teen needs to know you won't _____ during the difficult times.

Move from pleasing, protecting and providing, to _____ them for the future.

_____

_____

_____

_____

_____

_____

_____

_____

_____

©Copyright 2008. May not be copied without permission from the publisher. All rights reserved.

Understanding Your Teen

THIS WEEK'S FOCUS:

*Unconditional Love Creates the Arena for
Relationships that Meets Your Teenager's Longings
for Significance and Security*

Homework Day One

The Parenting Pendulum

Most of us in the mid-life years today grew up with parents who were influenced by a military mindset. Even earlier in our country's history, a farming economy, immigration to America and financial hardship caused by the Great Depression forced our ancestors to work hard for what they needed. The uncertainties of their time taught them the great value of protecting and providing for their families.

The parenting pendulum back then went far to the providing and protecting side. Parents focused on making certain there was enough food on the table and that their family was safe. Economic and military influences in place at the time brought families more personal discipline, more rigid rules, and more cultural sameness. Children understood what it meant to respect their parents.

Today, parenting styles have shifted, and family members relate to one another differently. The parenting pendulum has swung from the providing/protecting side to far the other way on the relational side. And while parents today tend to have better relationships with their kids, they often get less respect.

Also, the affluence in our culture has caused most teens to become more selfishly-motivated and more self-centered. The industrial and technological revolutions along with economic ease we experience allows parents to give kids more "stuff" than in any previous generation. And, since parents have it to give, we think that if we just give our kids everything they want, they will be happy. Parents give more and more, and expect little in return.

A Spoiled Generation

Think about it, did you have all the "stuff" your kids have when you were growing up? When I grew up, I had a stick! That was it! I began working for what I wanted in the fifth grade.

Some examples of what many kids have today that previous generations probably didn't have:

* A car on their 16th birthday
* IPOD or MP3 system, a personal DVD player
* The newest video games and movies
* Brand name clothes and shoes
* A cell phone, TV in their room, stereo-systems, computers, the Internet
* More free time than any other generation

What used to define a person – characteristics like honesty, obedience, and respect – are no longer the gold-standard. In today's world, a teen tends to define himself by what he has – the car, the IPOD, clothes, computers. Material things become the defining features of their lives

The problem? Teens tend to be naturally self-centered. No matter how much their parents give them, their attitude continues to be, "What *more* will you give me?" or "What do I get next?"

And, instead of working for what they want, they look to mom and dad, who willingly provide it. As a result, they don't appreciate what they have, and think of their parents as a money tree. If they don't get what they want, they may feel less acceptable to others, or may even become angry.

Yes, our generation has done a better job at developing relationships with our kids. Our generation's challenge, however, is to find better ways to teach kids how to successfully navigate life as responsible adults, and give them a sense of significance and security that has nothing to do with material possessions.

How does your parenting style differ from that of your own parents?

_____

_____

_____

Giving your teen more stuff doesn't necessarily mean they will be happier, feel more significant or help them become more responsible. It just means they have more, without understanding the sacrifice it took someone else to get it. Your teen won't learn the value of working for what they want if you continue to give them everything. And, your parenting pendulum must shift back toward helping them find out who they are and who they will be, and not always focus on their demands for more.

Identify some ways your child is overindulged or feels entitled?

_____

_____

_____

_____

_____

Look up this scripture: Proverbs 12:15 (NIV)

"The way of the _____ seems right to him, but a _____ man _____ to advice."

Overindulged teens eventually hit bottom, because they have nothing to look forward to. They already have it all! Unbridled spending by parents doesn't help a child. When real life calls, they are unprepared to answer. This is a foolish way to parent a child. So, instead of always providing or protecting – shift your focus to preparing them.

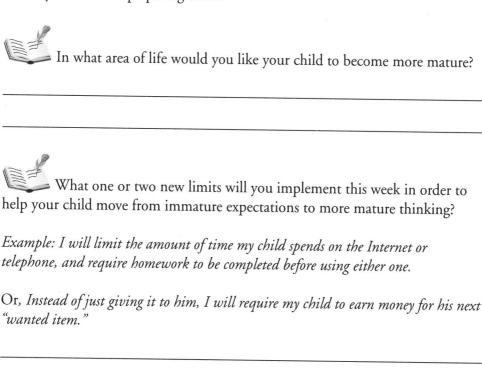 In what area of life would you like your child to become more mature?

_____

_____

What one or two new limits will you implement this week in order to help your child move from immature expectations to more mature thinking?

Example: I will limit the amount of time my child spends on the Internet or telephone, and require homework to be completed before using either one.

Or, *Instead of just giving it to him, I will require my child to earn money for his next "wanted item."*

_____

_____

Key Thought

Instead of always giving your kids everything they want, begin requiring them to find ways to work for it. It will prepare them for the future and give them a sense of accomplishment and appreciation for finances and material things that they won't otherwise learn.

Homework Day Two

When Parenting Moves to Peer-enting

Is it your goal in life to be your child's best friend? Out there on the far end of the relational spectrum are parents who place so much value on having a great relationship with their child that they do not take the appropriate position of authority in the life of their child.

When parents abandon their parental role to become more like their child's friend, they are more like a peer than a parent.

They're Not Parents, they are Becoming Peer-ents.

In an effort to build amiable relationships, peer-ents refrain from correcting or disciplining. Peer-ents have an intense need to be loved or accepted by their child, avoid conflict, and defend wrong behavior in order to remain on sociable terms. Peer-ents seek to have a child agree with them, and seek acceptance. Peer-ents won't correct a peer. Instead, a peer-ent will defend their child's actions to other parents, to teachers, or to law enforcement.

Look up this scripture: Proverbs 4:1 (NIV)

"Listen, my sons, to a father's _____ ; pay attention and

gain _____."

This scripture helps identify the role of a good parent: *Instruction* that leads a child to *understanding.*

Parenting Goal

The goal of parenting is to lead a child to godly thinking that results in godly behavior. The process may be more difficult than you first imagined. Getting the kind of understanding that leads to maturity takes refinement and discipline. It is something only a parent, not a peer-ent can offer. Your teen may not welcome the "instruction" or training, but he will someday thank you for the "understanding" he receives from it.

Like good exercise for the body, a godly parent willingly allows their child to experience some discomfort for a time in order to help them build their maturity muscles. The result of good discipline may mean your child is temporarily unhappy, and he may not like you in the process.

 How do you see yourself – are you acting as a parent should, or are you trying to be more like a peer? What about your child's other parent?

_____

_____

 Identify an area where you need to take more of an authoritative role in the life of your teen?

Example: I will say no when my child asks to watch a movie with inappropriate content, and I will not change my mind when my child is unhappy with my decision.

_____

_____

Key Thought

Your child needs you to be their parent, and not their peer. They have plenty of peers, but only you as their parent. If you don't help them move toward maturity and responsibility, no one else will. They are counting on you to discipline and train them to meet the demands of adulthood.

Homework Day Three

Longing for Significance and Security

A parent's role is to give their child a taste of the character of God that will be remembered throughout their life. God's character qualities are seen throughout the Bible, and there is no mistaking His love for us.

Look up this scripture: Jeremiah 31:3 (NIV)

"Jehovah has appeared to us in the past, saying; "I have loved you with an _____ _____ love; I have drawn you with _____- _____.

Definition of "Significance"
A realization of personal adequacy for a job which is truly important.

There are two things that last in this world, one is the Word of God, and the other is relationships. Both are eternal. As a child enters adolescence, their thinking changes from concrete to abstract. They move from a "doing" mindset to a "being" mindset.

At this stage, the secret longing of every child's heart is to belong in a relationship that helps them discover who they are, and who they will become. Your child realizes this sense of significance through relationships that will never end, first with you, here on Earth, and with God for all eternity.

Instilling Significance

Parents tend to play different roles in helping their child find significance. Moms instill a sense of value, and dads validate it. A child who doesn't experience a sense of significance in his relationships with his parents will search for it elsewhere – outside of mom or dad's influence.

You may even witness your child do unbelievably stupid or
dangerous things in order to find his sense of significance.

Your child may violate everything about his character until he finds the acceptance he longs for. And, the poor choices he makes often reaffirms or reinforces his childish thinking, childish behavior, and creates another problem – peer dependence.

Definition of "Security"

A convinced awareness of being unconditionally and totally loved without
needing to change in order to win love. The need to experience a love which
is freely given, cannot be earned, and therefore cannot be lost.

Building Security

Security means your teen knows that they don't need to perform in order to experience your unconditional love. Your relationship with them won't stop if they don't respond, or if they mess up. And, that your love survives during the tough times.

Their desire to be unconditionally loved and accepted is so intense,
they may violate their own values in order to find it elsewhere.

Memorize this Key Statement and Repeat It Daily to Your Teen

There is nothing you can do to make me love you more,
And there is nothing you can do to make you love you less.

Share the statement above with your child on a regular basis. Post it on your refrigerator door. Attach it to the bathroom mirror. Write it in soap on the windshield of their car. You cannot deliver this message to your teen too often. And, they need to hear it every day.

Having a relationship that offers significance and security means remaining involved in some way in their life. With acceptance and love, even when they mess up, you're preparing them to meet the challenges of their future adulthood.

What are some signs that your child has possibly lost a sense of significance or security in their life?

_____

_____

Where has your child's search for significance or security taken them – away from your family, or closer to your family?

_____

_____

How might you demonstrate unconditional love and personal acceptance to your child? (Be prepared to share them with your group.)

_____

_____

Key Thought

Your child will develop a sense of significance and security that comes from knowing they are valued by God, from your unconditional love, and by knowing they are an important member of your family. They need to sense that they "belong" regardless of what they look like, how well they do in school, what they own, or what they do.

Homework Day Four

10 Ways to Build (or Rebuild) Your Relationship

Yea, I have loved thee with an everlasting love: therefore
with loving-kindness have I drawn thee. —Jeremiah 31:3 (NIV)

Relationships thrive in settings where everyone agrees, "Nobody but God is perfect." In light of our imperfections, unconditional love is the key element to building any healthy relationship. God, our heavenly parent, models unconditional love throughout scripture.

Look up this scripture: I Corinthians 13: 4-8a (NIV)

(4) "Love is _____, love is _____. It does not envy, it does not boast, it is not _____. (5) It is not rude, it is not self-seeking, it is not easily _____, it keeps no _____ of _____. (6) Love does not delight in _____by rejoices with the _____. (7) It always _____, always _____, always _____, always perseveres. (8) Love never _____."

To create an arena in your home where a healthy relationship can develop, you must first have the kind of love that endures, and never ends.

Unconditional Love

A love that is delivered across a bridge of friendship,
which doesn't stop — even if one doesn't respond or makes a mistake.

How has your parenting style demonstrated something other than unconditional love to your child?

For Example: I am impatient with my child's bad habit, and I address it in anger instead of with kindness.

Read the following and consider how to implement some of these bridge-building opportunities with your teen:

10 Ways to Build a Sense of Significance and Security in Your Relationship

1. *By spending time together every week, one-to-one...*
Of all the advice I swear by, this is one you cannot ignore; Take your child out for breakfast, out for coffee, or do a lunch – every week. Make it a condition of getting allowance or going out on Friday night. Even if they resist, you insist. It tells your child, "You are worth spending time with, even when you are at your worst." Make it just you two.

2. *By sharing experiences...*
Find a challenge you both appreciate and pursue it with excitement. Dedicate some resources, time, effort, interest, and vigor to developing your interest together. Don't just send them, go with them.

3. *By looking for opportunities for discussion...*
Ask questions. Ask the kind of questions that make them think about things, not just a "yes" or "no" questions. Find out what they think, how they would do something, where they would go, why they think a certain way. Take advantage of those moments when a discussion leads to wisdom being shared along a common focal point.

Example 1: Attend a movie or play with an appropriate theme, and then follow up with a discussion about its moral principles…just ask and listen.

4. By listening more quickly and answering less often…

If you want to make your teen wonder what you are thinking, then stop telling him what you are thinking until he asks. Zip your lip – just be quiet. Stop lecturing, start listening. Don't tell them anything they've already heard you say a million times. Hush. I challenge you to try this for 24 hours and see what happens.

5. By developing a sense of humor…

Some of us are sour, bitter, and stressed all of the time. Lighten up! Try having a joke night – where everyone has to come to dinner with a joke to share. Even if it's corny or a little rank, everyone laughs! Take a vote and award the best laughs.

6. By having fun together…

Play paintball, rent a video, buy a music CD, go fishing, gaze at the stars, or pull a goofy stunt together. Get them up at midnight to watch the Northern Lights. Sleep in the woods, or camp on the beach. Live it up and enjoy life with your kids in some way, and work on your sense of humor while you're at it. If you don't like what they like, help them do more of what they like while you run the video camera.

7. By remembering your child's past and believing in your child's future…

Carry a photo of your child as a youngster with you at all times! Post it on your refrigerator. Take time to remember who this child was, and think about who he will become. Keep in mind the joy of bringing them home at birth. The thumbprint of God is still on their life. Don't dwell solely on their current struggles and difficulties. Thank God for the work He will do in your child's life.

8. By establishing boundaries…

Let them know where they can and can't "go" in your relationship. Tell them what you expect, before something challenges those expectations. Clearly establish your belief system and household rules. (See Lesson Six for more on Boundaries and Belief System for Discipline). Not establishing boundaries will hurt, not help.

9. By correcting and disciplining them, even when it makes you uncomfortable…

Choose your battles wisely, and seek the right things in your child's life for the right reason. Confront with calmness, correct with firmness, and with a love that seeks their best interest. Remember, discipline is discipleship for their good, not to make you feel better as a parent, or protect your reputation. Your child needs to know you love them enough to correct and discipline them when they behave in ways that offends others, breaks your household rules, offends God, or damages their relationships.

10. By acting on your faith and your beliefs…

Don't just say it, put your beliefs into action. Serve others, love others, forgive others, pray, worship. Exercise your faith in front of your child.

 Think about something you can discuss with your child. Take them out and listen to their ideas over a meal this week. Share with the group how it went.

Key Thought

The arena where relationships thrive consists of three main mandates:

1. Your teen knows you love them…
2. Your love is delivered across a bridge of friendship…
3. Your love <u>never</u> stops – even if your teen doesn't respond, shows nothing but hatred back toward you, or makes too many mistakes.

Building an arena for healthy relationships gives your child a taste of the character of God, and demonstrates that you love others in the same way God loves you.

Homework Day Five

The Commitment To Not Disengage

Look up this scripture: Proverbs 3:3 (NIV)

"Let love and faithfulness _____ _____ you; _____
them around your neck, _____ them on the tablet of your heart."

The teen years are not easy, for you or for them. Teens, by their very nature, are selfish and prone to making mistakes. They mess up, they blow it, they get into trouble, and they cause trouble.

Have you seen any of these actions or attitudes in your teen?

"The acts of the sinful nature are obvious: sexual immorality, impurity and debauchery; idolatry and witchcraft; hatred, discord, jealousy, fits of rage, selfish ambition, dissensions, factions and envy; drunkenness, orgies, and the like." –Galatians 5:19-21 (NIV)

Just as God hasn't abandoned us, a parent shouldn't abandon their teenager when they shows the signs of a sinful nature.

Have you made the commitment to stay engaged in your relationship with your teen, even when the going gets tough?

Will You Stay Engaged?

Will you stick with your teen even if she comes home pregnant, or your son wrecks the car? Even if they flunk a class or get caught shoplifting? Even if they use drugs, drink alcohol, lie to you, or cheat on a test? Do they know you will stick with them?

It takes commitment to not disengage, when disengaging
is the easiest thing to do.

No one is saying that there shouldn't be rules or consequences – not at all. Not disengaging means you also don't disengage from your parental role. And staying engaged means your child has room to make mistakes without losing his relationship with you, or suffering condemnation for making mistakes. There's a difference between condemnation (a judgment of character) and consequences (a tool to correct behavior).

The commitment to stay engaged:

- ♥ *Allows room for change, for both of you.*
- ♥ *Encourages and looks for something good in every situation, no matter how desperate.*
- ♥ *Is marked with kindness and tenderness*
- ♥ *Listens well and doesn't criticize, even when tired or discouraged.*
- ♥ *Displays strength when needed, and intervenes when necessary.*
- ♥ *Offers unconditional love and acceptance of the person, even when they mess up.*
- ♥ *Builds significance and security through a relationship that will never end.*
- ♥ *Doesn't give negative opinion or criticize everything they do.*
- ♥ *Doesn't operate out of fear or worry.*
- ♥ *Avoids the use of stinging words.*

Your relationship with your child allows you to communicate a better way of living, a different view of life, the need for a Savior, the Gospel of Christ, and a better perspective on how to live.

Does your relationship change when your child breaks the rules or doesn't measure up?

_____

_____

How might you develop a relationship with your child that moves him toward godly thinking and godly behavior, and offers him a sense of significance and security through unconditional love, acceptance, and friendship?

Example: I will not use anger as a tool to change their behavior, nor will I overlook it when he oversteps the boundaries.

_____

_____

Take time this week to tell your child, "There is nothing you can do to make me love you more, and there is nothing you can do to make me love you less."

Write down any response you receive from your child. Share how you feel about delivering that message with your group.

_____

_____

_____

Write a prayer and ask God for help in any of the areas we've discussed this week. Thank God for revealing areas you need to work on.

_____

_____

_____

Key Thought

Healthy relationships take work. It means being creative with the time you spend together, one-to-one. It takes commitment to stay engaged in the relationship, not condemning the teen – even when the going gets tough.

_____

_____

_____

_____

_____

_____

_____

_____

_____

_____

Heartlight

RESIDENTIAL COUNSELING CENTER FOR TEENS

For more information
about Heartlight, or to
receive an admission packet,
please call 903.668.2173
or visit our website at
www.HeartlightMinistries.org

AN ATMOSPHERE OF

relationships

Nestled among the beautiful piney woods of East Texas, Heartlight Ministries provides a residential counseling setting for adolescents in crisis situations. With a capacity for 48 co-ed residents, Heartlight offers intense, individual attention that fosters an atmosphere of relationships. This interaction with staff, residents and other families provides an arena for change and a chance to gain wisdom, support, and encouragement through difficult times.

When situations of divorce, death, abuse, social difficulties, academic struggles, adoption issues and unhealthy coping mechanisms (lying, selfishness, manipulation, entitlement, depression, lack of motivation, disrespect for authority, confusion) are present, Heartlight offers an answer when removal from the home is necessary. Founded in 1989, the Heartlight program has proven successful in the lives of hundreds of teens and their families.

CREATES AN ARENA FOR change

Understanding Your Parenting Role

My Lesson Notes
Understanding Your Parenting Role

(Fill in the blanks as underlined items show up on the video screen)

Perfect vs. Imperfect

A child's perception of their parents shifts during the adolescent years. Parents are no longer perfect in their eyes. Your teen begins to understand that he also is not perfect, and that those around him are not perfect, but that's okay.

You want your child to understand it is okay to _____ in life.

Let them know you aren't _____.

Affirm that it is okay to _____!

Struggle well _____!

The _____ they are projecting in their social circles usually is to _____ _____ _____ some struggle in their lives.

Is there something I _____ _____ know about my child that is affecting their _____?

Your teen's behavior is not a _____ of you, rather it's the display of the nature of man.

Your teen's behavior is often the result of facing some _____.

Home is to be the place the place to be the place of _____ and _____ _____ love.

Make you home an arena of shared _____, mutual respect and healthy _____.

Move your conversation from _____ to _____.

Move your conversation from _____ to _____ _____.

The power of a question: Instead of always giving _____, state a _____ _____that will make them think about it.

When you _____, your child will move toward you.

Move out of always solving their _____ and instead, allow them room to solve their own problems.

Give it _____ to them! We are too quick to take _____ for our teenager.

Give them _____ for their life choices.

Hold your _____ until they ask for it.

Welcome them by letting them know it is okay to _____ well.

Knowing that you are not a perfect parent gives your child hope for his own condition, and helps him understand his need for a Savior.

_____
_____
_____
_____
_____
_____
_____

©Copyright 2008. May not be copied without permission from the publisher. All rights reserved.

Understanding Your Parenting Role

> **THIS WEEK'S FOCUS:**
>
> *Successfully parenting adolescents means shifting your style of parenting from always doing everything for them, providing and protecting their every move, to preparing them to face the world in which they live.*

Homework Day One

Parents often wonder what they should do differently, but rarely consider how they need to "be" different.

Look up these scriptures: Isaiah 42:13 (NIV)

"Jehovah goes out as a _____ man. Like a _____ He will stir up His zeal; with a shout He will raise the battle cry and will triumph over His enemies."

Isaiah 66:13a (NIV)

"As a _____ _____ her child, so will I _____ you;"

These scriptures help define your two-fold role for parenting teens. The first goal is to give your child a sense of the true character of God by being what they need in a parent – as fearless as a warrior or as gentle and comforting as a mother.

The second goal involves shifting your style of parenting. The ideas and techniques you used eight years ago, when your child was four or five, don't work in the adolescent years. Your adolescent is discovering the world is no longer a perfect place. In fact, it's never perfect. You are not perfect, they are not perfect, and everyone around them has challenges and struggles.

Their Perceptions are Changing

Your child's perception of you is changing – right along with all of their physical, mental, and emotional changes. When they were younger, in their eyes, you could do no wrong. As they become teens, their perception of you changes to a new thought; "Everything you do is wrong!"

Adolescence moves your teen toward becoming an adult. As a new adult, they will have a new awareness of how relationships work. They will point out the problem areas, not only in your life, but in everyone else's life too! They will focus on your areas of conflict and irresponsibility. They will, sometimes with remarkable accuracy, tell how you really are, how you are perceived by others, and, what they think you need to do to become the perfect parent.

What they say may or may not be accurate. Even so, a humble willingness to admit your imperfections and to model change within your own life will model that we all need to learn to change gracefully.

Begin to show your teen that you are willing to hear criticism and listen to input, that you are not perfect, and you consider their point of view important and worth listening to. In turn, they'll do the same to you.

As your child moves into adolescence, how has his/her perception of you changed?

_____

_____

How are you adjusting your thinking to make room for "the new adult" in your household? For example: *I no longer walk into my child's room without first knocking.*

_____

_____

Give one practical example of how your parenting style needs to shift in order to meet your teen's changing perceptions? Be specific. Example: *I need to laugh more when my teen notices all my quirks when I drive the car. As long as he is not being disrespectful, I can admit my imperfections and laugh about them.*

_____

_____

Key Thought

Your teen's perception of you is changing. It is natural for them to think that everything you do is wrong! Admitting that you are not a perfect parent gives your teen a hopeful message; "Imperfection is a part of real life, and it's normal to not be perfect."

Homework Day Two

Engaging Your Teen in the Process of Life

As your style of relating to your teen changes, the way you handle their life's issues should move from handing out marching orders, and giving directives – always telling them what to do next – to engaging them in the process of life.

Begin by encouraging them to take on more responsibility; like getting themselves up in the morning for school, learning how to do laundry, caring for the family pet, or making more of the family decisions. Give them a checkbook, and money you would spend on their expenses, and teach them how to handle that money wisely. Let them choose where the family is going to eat, what movie to see, or where the family might go on their next vacation.

Handing responsibility over to your teen is difficult, and if you wait until you believe they are ready, you will never trust them to do more. Begin handing over some decisions even before you think they are ready for it, so they can begin to exercise their decision-making abilities.

Keep Quiet

Look up these scriptures: Proverbs 17:28 (NIV)

"Even a _____ is though wise if he keeps _____,
and _____ if he holds his tongue."

Proverbs 18:2 (NIV)
"A _____ finds no pleasure in understanding, but delights in airing his
own _____."

These scriptures define foolish behavior, and highlight an important way of teaching a teen to begin to think for himself. Quite simply, begin to remain quiet, and don't always give your teen your opinion or your advice. Don't remind them, lecture them, or advise them. Just keep quiet. They will be forced to think for themselves and come up with ideas and answers on their own.

Put even more simply, just listen to their ideas and feelings. It may be difficult to keep quiet when you hear their outlandish ideas and disagreeable thinking about things, but they won't be ready to hear your opinion unless they ask you for it. So don't offer it until they truly want to know what you think.

Wait to Be Invited

It's important to not give your advice until it's asked for. Even if it means your child may make a mistake.

It's never enjoyable to watch your child fail at something, but failure is not necessarily a bad thing when it causes your child to realize there's a problem with his choices. So, allow them the freedom to try something and to completely fail. Failure causes them to realize they need to ask for help. Allow your teen the opportunity to invite you to help them solve their problem, before you step in and fix everything for him.

Look for Opportunities for a Discussion

Look for opportunities to invite your teen into a discussion about life. Begin to ask more thought provoking questions. For example, ask them how they think something should be accomplished, and then listen to their opinion – without giving yours in return. Find out how they feel about things, or how they would approach solving a problem they are having. Asking questions helps a teen formulate opinions.

Don't Hover

Stop hovering over them when you've given them something to do. Give them an assignment and let them decide how to best get it done.

Instead of:
"Did you set your clock? You didn't get out of bed this morning in time for school. I told you to set your clock. You need to be out of bed by 6:30 or you won't make the bus on time. If the clock doesn't go off, you won't wake up."

Try:
Is there anything you need in the morning in order to get yourself up on time?
(Like an alarm clock!) Then, if they miss the bus, don't bail them out; let them come up with a reasonable solution for getting to school on time that doesn't inconvenience you. If they are late, they'll have to face the consequences.

Take the Focus off Performance

Change the focus of your parenting from how they perform (grades, sports, extra-curricular activities) to how they are developing in their character (honesty, trustworthiness, good life choices). Don't only focus on, "Did you pass your test," or "is your homework done?" Instead, force them to participate in your relationship by talking about their thoughts, feelings, and ideas. That will only happen if you spend time together.

Instead of only:
"Did you pass your test today?" Or, *"Why weren't you able to score better than 70% on your test today? Is your homework finished? Did you feed the cat? Why didn't you make captain of the team?"*

Try talking about:
"Is there anything you don't like about school? How does earning your own money make you feel? What would make our home a better place to live? What is it about drama class you love so much? What do you think it will take to live on your own someday? How do you think I should respond when you are disrespectful to me? If you were in my shoes, what would you do?"

Do you "tell" your child what to do, or "engage" your teen in the process of life and making decisions?

_____

_____

Think of some of the questions you currently ask your child, and write down some new questions to better engage their thinking as replacements: Example: *Performance-based relationships focus on "what you do" or "how well did it" Character-based relationships focus on the character of the person and what they are thinking.*

_____

_____

Is it difficult for you to allow your child to make a decision and fail, in order to help him learn how learn a better way the next time?

_____

_____

What will shift in order to allow your child to take more responsibility for his decisions? For Example: *If my child fails a class in school, it will be up to him to figure out how to make up the credit. I will no longer push them.*

_____

_____

🔑 Key Thought

Begin giving your teen more opportunities to make their own decisions. Keep quiet, and wait until they ask for your help or invite your opinion before giving it. Begin to ask questions that focus on how they feel about things, or their ideas, and less about how they perform. Allow them to fail.

Homework Day Three

My Child's Relational Style

Look up this scripture: Luke 6:44 (NIV)

"Each tree is _____ by its own _____. People do not pick figs from thorn-bushes, or grapes from briers."

This scripture helps us see that each child is unique, and responsive to the influences around them. The key to knowing the heart of your child comes from understanding their difficulties and struggles as **they** perceive them. It helps a parent understand why they act they way they do.

What is a relational style?

"The characteristic manner of offering and protecting oneself in social interactions. It is the expression of one's personality through a calculated presentation of one's self."

Unless there is some sort of great dysfunction at home during a child's early years, younger children don't much care what anyone thinks of them. They are carefree. As maturing teens, however, that sense of carelessness turns into intense self-scrutiny, and brutal self-awareness, partly because their peers begin competing with them. Their heightened sense of self causes them to project what they feel they need to project in order to be accepted by others (especially their peers). When a teen chooses a particular way to behave in order to find acceptance among his peers, this is the teen's relational style.

Understanding your child's unique relational style as they evolve from childhood to adulthood helps explain why you are beginning to see behavior in your teen that is unlike what you've seen in them before. There is no right or wrong relational style. It is what it is, and a parent needs to learn how to relate to it.

A teen's relational style develops in response to things that have impacted their lives:

- ♥ *They feel unaccepted or different, and are seeking acceptance from their peers.*
- ♥ *They could have experienced a loss or change (a friend's death, a medical problem, a divorce, victimization).*
- ♥ *They feel a sense of rejection (this happens often with adopted children).*
- ♥ *To accommodate for a problem in the family (in my family, we always needed to be right).*
- ♥ *Because they don't know how to fit in, but desperately want to.*

As parents, we tend to focus on our child's new "behavior," and can consider it their "misbehavior." The secret to making a successful transition from parenting pre-teens to parenting teenagers is to take the focus off of their behavior, and begin to understand their relational style.

Your teen's changing behavior is often a result of some personal difficulty they are facing, and he or she may be struggling as a result. The key is to discern what is affecting their unique soul, and look at the secondary symptoms in a wider context – their style of relating.

Parents Need to Be Aware if these Potential Causes of Unusual Behavior

- ✓ *DISCONNECTION: They may be trying to deal with a sense of feeling unaccepted and disconnected from everyone around them.*
- ✓ *CRUELTY: They may be protecting themselves from cruelty, abuse, or from feeling further hurt.*
- ✓ *LOW SELF-ESTEEM: They may be manipulative and lie in order to feel esteemed, and appear to be right at any cost.*
- ✓ *INNOCENCE: They may be covering up a loss of innocence.*
- ✓ *MEDICAL: They may be compensating for a medical problem, like ADHD or depression.*
- ✓ *SHAME: They may feel shame or guilt over making a wrong decision.*
- ✓ *ABANDONMENT: They may be trying to overcome feelings of abandonment.*
- ✓ *LOSS OF FAITH: They may be choosing to be self-willed and self-directed because they have lost their trust in God.*

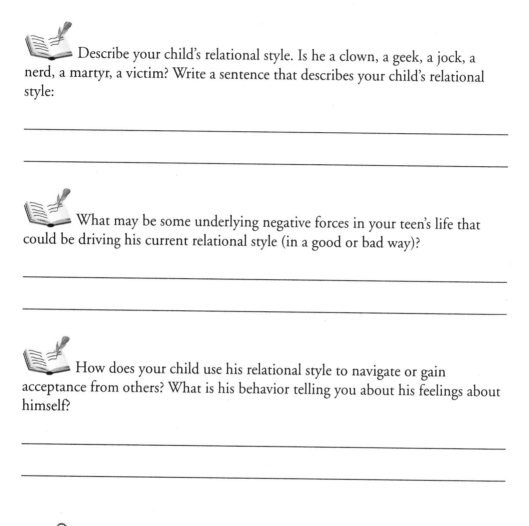

Describe your child's relational style. Is he a clown, a geek, a jock, a nerd, a martyr, a victim? Write a sentence that describes your child's relational style:

_____

_____

What may be some underlying negative forces in your teen's life that could be driving his current relational style (in a good or bad way)?

_____

_____

How does your child use his relational style to navigate or gain acceptance from others? What is his behavior telling you about his feelings about himself?

_____

_____

Key Thought

As you begin to understand your child's relational style, you see how they project themselves to others in order to compensate for things they feel as damage or loss. At all costs, seek to identify and understand the negative forces that drive their behavior, and respect your child for the difficulties they face in their everyday world. Don't allow them to get away with bad behavior (apply appropriate consequences), but take a moment to understand where it may be coming from.

Homework Day Four

Offering Rest for Their Soul

Look up this scripture: Matthew 11:28 (NIV)

"Come unto me all ye who are _____, and _____ and I will give you _____."

Do you perceive that adolescence is easy for your teen? Do you surmise that you know everything that is happening in your child's life? Do you think your child's burden is light? Parents don't often realize the difficulties teens face, and we can trivialize their problems, which to them may seem to be "life and death" issues. But we often offer a "just get-over-it" mentality. An encouraging, safe, and secure relationship is just the refuge your child needs as he goes through the turbulent waters of adolescence

Imagine what a restful place is like, and compare it to the atmosphere you create when your child comes to you with a problem he is facing, or after making a mistake.

Look up this scripture: James 1:19b (NIV)

"Everyone should be quick to _____, slow to _____, and slow to become _____."

When a teen struggles, they rarely seek out their parents' help. So when your teen, who may already be struggling, comes to you, do they:

- ♥ *Face a barrage of critical words and angry responses?*
- ♥ *Leave more worn out or more refreshed?*
- ♥ *Feel more shame than hope?*

- ♥ *Feel embraced or embarrassed?*
- ♥ *Leave "less understood" or leave "more understood."*
- ♥ *Find a safe haven or a boxing ring?*

Parents often ask, "How can I offer comfort and embrace my teen, and still be the disciplinarian, the authority, and the goal-keeper?" It requires a two-fold approach: Both, standing behind them, in support of them, and heading them in a direction they want to go. And, standing in front of them to stop them from moving in a direction that may damage their life or end up in a place they don't want to be.

What do your current reactions convey to your teen when they are burdened? Are you a "brick wall" or "a soft place to fall?"

_____

_____

What will you change in the way you handle your child's difficulties in order to let them know you want to hear and understand their struggles?

_____

_____

Most kids will say they want to "be like" someone, more than they want to "do" what others are doing. Who would you most like your child to "be like" by the time he is an adult?

_____

_____

 What can you do to make your home a more attractive place for your teen to find "rest" for his soul?

_____

_____

Key Thought

Give your teen all the time and attention they need in order to work through a problem, without responding with criticism and anger. This may mean allowing them to experience the appropriate consequences without bailing them out, while encouraging them at the same time. Be quick to listen, slow to speak, slow to anger. Offer rest for their weariness by understanding the relational difficulties they face on a daily basis. React to their struggles in a way that eases their burden instead of adding to it.

Homework Day Five

Being Who God Has Called Me to Be

The way you handle your relationship with your teen at this time of their life will determine whether you will be rubbing shoulders with them and having a good relationship ten or twenty years from now.

Look up this scripture: Philippians 2:3 (NIV)

"Do nothing out of _____ _____ or _____

_____, but in humility consider others _____ than yourselves."

The Bible instructs every believer to consider others as more important than themselves. In parenting, especially when it comes to solving problems or addressing areas of struggle, it's good to deal with your child as more important than yourself. Keep in mind that discipline is for their benefit. It is not meant to be punishment, though it will seem that way to the teen. Discipline includes training, and is not just to help you feel better about being a good parent.

Look up this scripture: Proverbs 22: 6 (NIV)

"_____ up a child in the way he should go, and when he is old he will not turn from it."

Parenting involves training. Not just spiritual training, but preparation for the world in which they must live. That includes managing money, driving a car, interacting with friends, serving others, taking care of belongings, working for what they want, and living within society's laws and healthy expectations.

Name five ways you are training your child to navigate in the world in which he lives:

1. _____

2. _____

3. _____

4. _____

5. _____

Name five areas you haven't trained your child in, but would like to begin; For example, "I need to teach my child how to manage a checkbook and spend money wisely." Write down how you will accomplish this training.

1. _____

2. _____

3. _____

4. _____

5. _____

Don't Be Distracted

It's easy to become distracted by a host of other issues, and miss the heart of your child when they share their struggles with you. Remember to open yourself up and embrace their struggles, offer them hope, and be present and in the moment with them. Give them kindness, love, and compassion, even when they've messed up. And part of compassion, whether it seems like it or not, is to not back off on applying consequences.

Has your idea of discipline and parenting your teen changed as a result of this week's study? If so, how?

_____

_____

What three areas of change would you like to work on first? Mark them.

☐ Keeping silent more instead of lecturing.

☐ Allowing my child to experience failure.

☐ Training my child to make decisions for himself.

☐ Understanding my child's world more.

☐ Considering their struggles as more important than my ideas.

☐ Developing questions for good discussion.

☐ Admitting my own mistakes or failures.

☐ Staying engaged when my child struggles (including making mistakes).

☐ Becoming more quick to listen, and slow to anger.

Specifically, how do you plan to accomplish these things this week? (Share these with your group).

_____

_____

Key Thought

Your role as a parent is to give your child a taste of the character of God, and it involves more than just doing, it involves "being." Be who God has called you to be as their parent. Point them to God, and live out your beliefs with humble conviction. Understand your child's heart, and consider them as "more important" when dealing with their mistakes or failures.

©Copyright 2008. May not be copied without permission from the publisher. All rights reserved

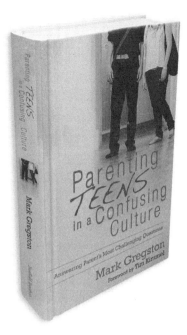

HAVE YOU SEEN
the effects of this confusing culture on your teen?

DO YOU EVER WONDER
if today's teen culture will affect your child?

ARE YOU CONFUSED
trying to navigate in these waters called adolescence?

Teen expert Mark Gregston answers 32 of the toughest questions asked by today's parents concerning their teen, and gives solid insight and practical wisdom on how to approach your teen during the time of their life that they need you the most. Mark shares stories of more than 2,000 teens that have lived with him, and the lessons that he has learned from his involvement in their lives. Whether you have a teen who is struggling, are fearful that your teen might struggle when they enter the teen years, or just want to prepare now for those often turbulent years, this book is for you.

"Mark has a clear, 'big picture' grasp of effective parenting. It's formatted by the power of God's grace and seasoned from decades of experience."

–DR. TIM KIMMEL, President, Family Matters

To purchase this book, visit heartlightresources.org or your local bookstore.

Understanding Your Teen's Behavior

My Lesson Notes
Understanding Your Teen's Behavior

(Fill in the blanks as underlined items show up on the video screen)

All behavior is _____ _____.

Definition of a "Need:"

Those perceived, real, or convinced conditions, possessions, environments, relationships or actions that are essential required or desired to fill or obscure an area where something is _____ or _____.

Some of your child's needs may be the result of _____ in his/her life.

Definition of a "Loss:"

Something that _____ _____, that isn't.
Something that _____ _____ _____, but is not.

A child doesn't move to abnormal behavior without first _____ _____.

Help your teen know it is okay to be "_____" by sharing your _____ with them.

Losses are something a parent usually cannot _____.

"Don't grow weary in _____ _____, for in due time you will _____ if you surely sow." – Galatians 6:9 (NIV)

Move _____ your child when you see the _____, even if they are doing everything wrong.

A mother instills a _____ ____ _____ in a child.

Teens will find _____ in any way they can and with whomever will _____ _____.

"Lord, search me, know my _____ and see if there is any ____ _____ _____ in me; and _____ me in the way everlasting. – Psalm 139:23-24 (NIV)

Give kids license to _____, but not license to _____ _____ _____.

There are no _____ in scripture for parenting teen difficulties.

Behavior is not the problem…the _____ _____ the behavior is what needs to be addressed.

Be there for them…speak the _____ in love during difficult times.

Notes

_____

_____

_____

_____

_____

_____

_____

©Copyright 2008. May not be copied without permission from the publisher. All rights reserved.

Understanding Your Teen's Behavior

> **THIS WEEK'S FOCUS:**
>
> *The key to explaining their behavior, and why they act the way they do, lies in understanding the hidden motivation of a teen's heart.*

Homework Day One

Mysterious Behavior Unraveled

All teenage behavior is goal-oriented, and it doesn't always make sense. You probably already agree that your teen's behavior doesn't always make sense. In fact, most of the time it doesn't make any sense! You may ask, "Why does my child act that way?" Or, "Why am I having such a hard time understanding what my child wants?"

Every teen longs for something. You have to begin with what they long for:

- ♥ They want someone to hear what they are saying.
- ♥ They want someone to notice them.
- ♥ They want to show their maturity and independence.
- ♥ They want to cover up the pain of abuse or trauma.
- ♥ They want to feel accepted.
- ♥ They want to know that they are more than the rejection they feel.
- ♥ They want find peace and relief.

A teen will use his relationships to accomplish one important goal: finding significance outside of home. Sometimes a child's motivation to do a negative thing is rooted in something that is actually very good. Sometimes they just want in their life to be different.

When trying to understand your teen's behavior, take time to examine their hidden motivations. Don't be distracted by the way they behave, and don't focus on their missteps. Instead, begin to understand their heartfelt longings, and learn how to respond with sensitivity.

Look up this scripture: Psalm 139:14a (NIV) What does it say about your teen's unique soul?

"I will give thanks to Thee, for I am _____ and _____ _____ made."

Their Unique Behavior Strategy

God made your child with a unique soul, a unique personality, and individuality. Your child has a "unique behavior strategy" – yes, there is a strategy behind his behavior, and it is unique to his own soul. His behavior is a reflection of his longings and his personality.

What Does Your Child Want?

Each child's personal behavior strategy takes focus and intensity to understand. To find significance, one child may choose drugs, another may drink, or another may seek academic accomplishment, popularity, or good looks. Yet another may intentionally flunk and hang with the "out" crowd, because they are the most accepting. Girls may use their physical power to attract, and guys may choose athletics or their car as the way to find acceptance.

You may ask, "What could possibly be the motivation for my child to take up drinking? What does my child get from smoking dope; isn't his life pretty easy? Why does my daughter behave so seductively; is she sexually active now? What's up with my son flunking out of school? Whatever made my child think that shoplifting was okay? Why does my child lie all the time?"

Teens are relational beings. They want to have relationships with others, and feel valued by them. In fact, they long for it. They will use their relationships to feel more connected. Your child may "try on" many different personas, and different related behaviors, until they find the one that "fits" their need to feel connected.

Feeling connected and accepted is a strong need, and your child may behave in ways that violate his or her own values, or go against everything you taught them in order to make that connection with someone else. Unfortunately, a struggling teen may not even know what their unique goal is. Usually, the more bizarre their behavior, the more desperate a teen is to achieve that goal.

What in your child's behavior concerns you the most right now?

_____

_____

What could your child's behavior be telling you about his search for significance or security?

_____

_____

In what ways is your child fearfully and wonderfully made, or unique?

_____

_____

Homework Day Two

Understanding Your Child's Needs

Look up this scripture: Luke 15:14 (NIV)

"After he had spent everything, there was a _____ _____
in that whole country, and he began to be in _____."

The Prodigal

The story Jesus told of the Prodigal Son says he spent everything he had on riotous living, and when famine came to the land he began to be in need. Eventually his need turned into desperation – causing him to come to a different conclusion about the way he was living. His need caused him to make a better choice in life.

Likewise, <u>your</u> teen's behavior is determined by what he perceives he needs.

From the video lesson this week, remember the definition of a need?

Definition of "Need:"
Real, perceived, or convinced conditions,
possessions, environments, relationships, or actions
that are essential, required, or desired
to fill or obscure an area where something
is lacking or unattainable.

Unmet needs in your teen's life are addressed or managed by his choices. The prodigal's unmet need to fill his stomach caused him to reconsider the way he was living. He came to his senses and returned to his father's house, seeking forgiveness. His lifestyle choices changed in order to meet his needs.

For example, anyone can predict what will happen when they drink too much water. They'll need to find the restroom. If someone stops them, or gets in their way, they'll behave more intentionally in order to meet their need. Or, they'll find another way to meet the need. They won't stop until their need is met.

Your teen may be acting the way he does because of an unmet need. Outside of the obvious – the need to feel loved and accepted – he may have an unmet need you don't understand. Perhaps he just needs to feel "normal," because things at home aren't normal. He may feel stressed all the time and just need to learn how to relax, and laugh more. He may need to grieve a death, or the breakup of the family, or deal with being abused or the loss of a friend.

If he perceives his needs will not be met within his current setup, he'll find another way. If something is in the way of meeting his needs, like your household rules or behavior mandates, he'll go around them. If he can't find what he feels he needs at home, he'll search for it outside the home. If the frustration of unmet needs continues to grow, your teen will move in unhealthy directions in order to feel find relief.

I often tell parents of teens, if they are hungry enough, they'll eat anything, and it will taste good. If your teen is relationally hungry enough, don't be surprised to find them involved in ways that may surprise you, shock you, or dismay you.

On the following list, mark some of your child's greatest needs right now:

☐ Needs to feel in control
☐ Needs to overcome guilt
☐ Needs to feel accepted
☐ Needs better self-esteem
☐ Needs medical issues resolved
☐ Needs to accept others
☐ Needs to deal with victimization
☐ Needs to grieve
☐ Needs to be believed
☐ Needs to be physically fit
☐ Needs to be right all the time

☐ Needs to overcome shyness
☐ Needs to overcome loneliness
☐ Needs to feel more loved
☐ Needs to feel more normal
☐ Needs lots of activity
☐ Needs to vent
☐ Needs to feel smarter
☐ Needs to feel prettier
☐ Needs to feel more popular
☐ Needs to overcome the loss of a parent or friend.

Value and Validation from Mom and Dad

Most kids feel comfortable sharing life's deeper issues with Mom more than they do with Dad. They also feel they can express their anger (sometimes very appropriately) to a mom, because moms usually don't seek to distance themselves from what's happening in a teen's life. Moms tend to hang in there, no matter what. Moms, in this way, instill value in their child. If mom is absent or removed, a child tends to feel unvalued.

Dads, on the other hand, often put distance in their relationships. And when a dad is absent, or removed from the relationship altogether by divorce, death, or in some other way, problems with a teen often follow.

Why?

> *Because moms tend to instill a sense of value in a child,*
> *and dads are the ones who validate it.*

Children need a father's 'stamp of approval.' When Dad's stamp of approval is missing, a child will look for validation somewhere else. Dad, you are the most influential person in your child's life. More than anything, outside of their relationships with God, your child needs <u>your</u> stamp of approval.

Who fulfilled the role of instilling a sense of value in your life? How did they communicate value to you?

_____

_____

What can you do to communicate a sense of value (Moms) or give your child your stamp of approval (Dads) this week?

_____

_____

Homework Day Three

Identifying Loss in the Life of Your Child

Loss in the life of a teen is like is an empty space in their heart, and they want it filled. If you fill it with something other than what they really long for, they won't want it. **Even if those other things are just as good.**

Think about a child who has lost a parent through death or divorce – or even an adopted child. Your child feels the loss of their birth parent. There may be nothing wrong with the replacement, but replacements will always be that, not the authentic original. Your child longs to not have that loss, at all, and every time they are around the replacement, they are reminded of what they no longer have.

If your child is adopted, then every normal family is a reminder to your child that his is a "different" kind of family. It doesn't matter if you are a good parent, or not. You could be giving him everything he wouldn't have had. Even so, you are a reminder that his birth-mother gave him up, which is not what your child may have wanted. He may never have wanted to be adopted.

Losses tend to control us by the needs they create. They are either real or perceived.

Broader definition of a "Loss:"
Not getting what I want, need, or hope for...
(For instance: the boyfriend or girlfriend, the job, the car, the recognition.)
that which I am deprived of, fail to take advantage of, or defeated by...
(For instance: missed opportunities, parental expectations, bad decisions, an inability to do what I think I should be able to do.)
that which I am unable to maintain or keep...
(For instance: my parent's marriage, my friendships, my popularity.)
that which I am unable to find...
(For instance: peace with siblings, a group of friends to hang out with, other kids like me, a cure.)
that which I fail to win...
(For instance: my parent's attention, the heart of a girl, the applause of my peers.)
that which once was, but now isn't.
(For instance: a sense of safety, divorce or death, sexual purity, faith, attending my favorite school.)

There are many ways your teen may experience loss: Through the actions of others, unavoidable circumstances, irresponsible care-giving, lawless disobedience, prejudice, or generational sickness. In any event, when there is a loss, there is also a feeling that their life is out of control.

Or, perhaps your teen has experienced the negative effects of unmet expectations, not being heard or understood, not being loved and cared for, or not feeling valued or esteemed.

Perhaps your teen has unfulfilled dreams, has missed goals or opportunities, or longs for something unattainable.

Or, maybe they feel loss from uncontrolled happenings, and inherited affliction, a medical problem, something about their appearance, or where they live bothers them.

The intensity in your teen's behavior, good or bad, grows as they pursue their goals. They become 'bent" on getting what they want. Most people would say, "Let them have it and then they'll learn it's not true." But in these days the resulting consequences can be dangerous, or life-changing.

In light of this new understanding of how loss affects a teen, tell of a time when you asked, "Why is my child acting like that" and how a loss may have fueled their behavior?

_____

_____

What can you do this week to help your child effectively deal with his sense of loss, his need, and his resulting behavior?

_____

_____

Homework Day Four

How Teens Respond To Loss

A child doesn't move to behaving abnormally without first experiencing loss.

Every child is unique in the way they respond to their losses. But let me list four of the most common responses to loss:

1. Anger

Anger is the number one response to loss. When teens perceive a loss, the void is often filled with frustration or anger.

Anger is the emotional response to not getting what you want, even if you don't exactly know you're not getting what you want.

The more intense the loss, the more desperate their behavior, and greater their anger. When you intervene in the life of your child in order to curb their inappropriate or unacceptable behavior, your child will become even angrier. No one likes to be told, "No."

2. Minimizing

"It's not that big of a deal." Minimizing their loss reduces the importance of their loss so it won't demand anyone's attention. Or, they may act as if it didn't happen, and convince themselves that everything is really "okay." Minimizing is not dealing with the loss and may delay or cover it up until it explodes.

3. Guilt

Another common response to loss is guilt. They have an ongoing sense of regret, and feel terrible about something that's happened, or something they've done or they may blame themselves. They avoid dealing with it, especially if they were part of creating the loss to begin with. Underneath this thinking is the belief that dealing with their loss may cause something else in their life to fall apart, resulting in additional loss. When one domino falls, it knocks down the rest of the dominoes too. Instead, they just feel guilty.

4. Shame

"I'm embarrassed that I couldn't handle it." They may wonder why they aren't equipped to deal with it, or why they didn't see what would happen before it happened. Underneath this thinking is a belief that they should be able to take care of everything on their own, and know what to do every time trouble appears.

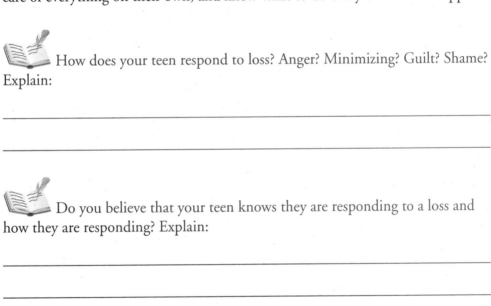 How does your teen respond to loss? Anger? Minimizing? Guilt? Shame? Explain:

_____

_____

Do you believe that your teen knows they are responding to a loss and how they are responding? Explain:

_____

_____

As the parent of a teen, you are in a unique position to help your child by looking beyond the way they are behaving, by examining their needs and understanding their losses.

Uncovering Loss

A 16-year-old boy's life was torn apart when it was discovered by his parents that he had been drawn into a sexual relationship with a 23 year-old female – who was also his high school teacher. His parents expressed disbelief in their son's ability to hide such happenings from them. They knew something was wrong, but attributed the trouble with their son's behavior to raging hormones and normal teen angst.

Bewildered at finding out the truth, they asked their son, "Why didn't you ever tell us what was happening to you?" Their son simply responded, "Why didn't you ever ask ?"

Parents often don't like to ask such tough questions as, 'Has anyone ever said or done anything that was inappropriate to you?" Parents often focus on their teen's behavior by simply overlooking the obvious, or by attributing their teen's difficult behavior to other things – bad friends, problems in school, experimenting with drugs, even outright rebellion.

> *Do your parents know everything that happened*
> *in your life during your teen years? Probably not!*
> *Then, what makes you think you know everything that*
> *is happening in your own teen's life?*

If you see a drastic, unexplainable change in your child's behavior, something else is going on, underneath it, fueling it. It's important to ask, and keep asking until you are satisfied you understand what is happening in the life of your child. It may not be sexual abuse, but it may be something else just as traumatic to your child's unique soul.

Old Patterns

A frustrated step-father was fed up with his step-son's abuse of their family. This son constantly used his mother's guilt over the divorce against her, and milked it for all it was worth. Mom constantly caved. She bailed him out, gave him money, let him live at home – even when he was disrespectful to her and everyone else. She paid his traffic fines, spoke to school officials on his behalf, and didn't say much when things went missing from her home. Instead of requiring her son to respect and obey her, despite his anger, she hid behind a covering of shame and guilt. The losses in her own life rendered her inactive in her role as a parent, and her son developed abusive habits as a result.

Your own losses often shape your relationships, including the one with your child. Are your own losses getting in the way of being the kind parent God called you to be – one that speaks truth and gives grace?

How might your responses to your own losses be affecting how you parent your teen?

_____

_____

Key Thought

Your role in godlike parenting requires truth and grace. There is a tough and tender side to being a good parent. Sometimes the truth is painful, but your child needs you to be strong enough to be truthful in responding to bad behavior. The graceful side of parenting means you understand your child longings, and move toward him with compassion during the tough times.

Homework Day Five

What God Promises About Loss

Look up this scripture: Romans 8:28-29a (NIV)

"And we know that in all things God works _____ of those who love Him, who have been called according to His purpose. For those God foreknew He also predestined to be conformed to the _____ of His Son..."

What do these verses say about how God promises to use our losses? What is His ultimate goal?

_____

_____

Isaiah 61:3 (NIV)

"...to bestow on them a _____ instead of _____, the oil of gladness instead of mourning, and a garment of praise instead of a spirit of despair. They will be called oaks of righteousness, a planting of the LORD for the display of His splendor."

Using the Children of Israel as an example, this verse says God replaces ashes with _____. God replaces mourning with _____. God gives a garment of _____to replace despair.

God uses loss to make you more like Him, to glorify Him, and to acknowledge His goodness in your life. God promises He will fill the empty spaces left by losses. But, it may not happen on your timetable. Most likely, it won't happen on your timetable.

Write a prayer asking God to help you identify your child's losses and understand your child's heartfelt longings.

_____

_____

_____

_____

_____

Key Thought

During adolescence, teens are caught in the "Muddle in the Middle." They have little ability to understand that God promises to recover them from loss. It is not something they can fully embrace until they are adults. Parenting a child who has experienced deep loss is a matter of waiting and watching for God to use every situation for His good in both your life, and the life of your child.

Looking for help with your teen?

Mark Gregston's book *When Your Teen is Struggling* brings hope and direction to families looking for help with their out-of-control teen. The book has been a welcome word to weary hearts. A recent review by Armchair Interview states, "If the world of advice for parents of teenagers is a vast ocean, then Mark Gregston's book, *When Your Teen Is Struggling*, is an island that rises above."

Armchair further states, "It's rare when a self-help book is hard to put down. Gregston draws you in with heartfelt stories that are sometimes horrifying, sometimes amazing, but always intriguing. When you've finished reading the book, you'll surely want to tell a friend about it. It's that kind of book."

"Gregston draws you in with heartfelt stories that are sometimes horrifying, sometimes amazing, but always intriguing." Armchair Review

To purchase this book, visit heartlightresources.org or your local bookstore.

Understanding Your Relationship

My Lesson Notes
Understanding Your Relationship

(Fill in the blanks as underlined items show up on the video screen)

Performance-Based Relationships...tend to be _____ and convey or withholds love based on _____.

We all long to be _____ _____.

"Performance-Oriented" means I long for _____ _____ for you.

"Performance-Oriented" means not tying _____ _____ to performance.

Your home needs to be a place of _____ and _____, not _____.

There's much more to education than _____.

Help your kids be _____.

Teenage fads _____ soon enough.

In the bigger scheme of things, _____ _____ don't matter.

How you respond to _____ _____ is how they will later respond to you if they become like _____ _____.

Rules set the standards...but to be effective the must be _____.

"Grace" is giving them something they _____ _____.

Rules without _____ causes rebellion.

"Mercy" is _____ getting something that you _____ _____.

If you expect _____ _____…you'll have disappointment, discouragement, despair and despondency from your child.

If you expect too little…you'll have a child that is _____ and feels like a

_____.

Communicate _____ _____.

Notes

_____

_____

_____

_____

_____

_____

_____

_____

_____

_____

_____

©Copyright 2008. May not be copied without permission from the publisher. All rights reserved.

Understanding Your Relationship

THIS WEEK'S FOCUS:

God is the only perfect being. So, don't expect perfection, don't project that you are perfect, and don't project that your kids need to be perfect.

Homework Day One

Performance-Based Patterns

Definition: A performance-based relationship determines a person's value by a particular action, accomplishment or achievement.

The pattern for performance-based relationships begins when a child is young and parents convey the message; "When you do something you shouldn't, you get into trouble. When you do what you should, you get rewarded. Further, I'm happier with you when you do what you should."

As the child moves toward becoming a teen, he naturally begins to fear losing your approval when he disobeys. He fears losing your love when he doesn't meet your expectations. He fears losing his place in youth group or with his peers because of his struggles. His sense of security is in question when it looks like you are willing to walk away when he is going through a tough time. If he tries and it is deemed not good enough, then he'll eventually give up and say, "What's the use trying?"

Do any of the following patterns resemble your relationship with your child?

Do you....

* *Find it difficult to remain emotionally available to your child when their behavior disappoints you?*
* *Try to shame or embarrass your child into doing what you think he should?*

* *Isolate your child, or make your child eat meals in another room until he meets with your expectations (grades, homework, chores)?*
* *Shun or refuse to spend time with him because of his wrongdoing or mistake?*
* *Verbally express extreme frustration and make your child feel he can't do anything right?*
* *Nag your child about his bad habits or focus on his flaws?*
* *Let him suffer consequences without your support or kindness, or worse yet, with what seems to be your pleasure in handing out consequences?*

If you recognize yourself in any these areas, you may have a performance based relationship.

Without realizing it, you may be sending him the message, "If you don't perform up to my standards, then you won't have my love."

Look up these scriptures: Genesis 1:27 (NIV)

"So God created man in His _____ _____, in the image of _____ _____ created him; male and female He created them."

Genesis 5:1 (NIV)

"This is the written accounts of Adam's line. When God created man, He made him in the _____ of God."

How might knowing your child is created in God's own image, and not yours, affect your relationship with your teen?

_____

_____

Remember…your teenager needs to often hear you say:

There is NOTHING you can do to make me love you more,
and NOTHING you can do to make me love you less.

Assignment:

What is your child's perception of your relationship right now? Your child's perception of how you feel about him is important. Don't hesitate to ask your teen his view of your relationship. Take him out to breakfast and ask,

"Do you believe there is anything that you could
do that would make me love you less?"

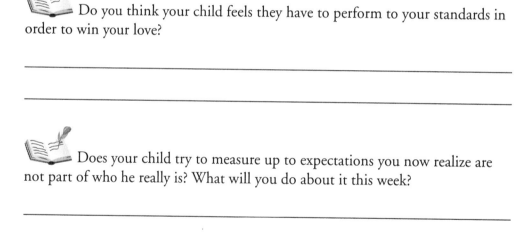 Do you think your child feels they have to perform to your standards in order to win your love?

_____

_____

Does your child try to measure up to expectations you now realize are not part of who he really is? What will you do about it this week?

_____

_____

Key Thought

If your child feels there is something they could do to lose your love, begin a conversation about how you can begin to communicate your unconditional love instead.

Homework Day Two

Areas of Performance-Based Parenting

It's easy to love someone when they agree with you, and difficult when they don't.

As your teen enters adolescence and turns into a completely jumbled up, disagreeable, emotional mess, he longs for the assurance that you love him – not only when he is doing well, but also when he is not.

As was discussed in Day One, a performance-based relationship means your child believes, "My parents won't like me anymore if I do the wrong thing." Or, "My parents won't help me unless I do what they expect."

There are many areas where performance can become the focus of your relationship with your teen. Remember, we're talking bout teenagers, not younger children. Here are some of the most common areas where performance can be overly emphasized:

* **Academic or educational pursuits**

Is getting good grades, passing every class, getting all A's, pursuing the right degree, attending the college you approve more important than valuing your child for who he is and what he wants to pursue educationally?

* **Dress or appearance**

Has embarrassment about the way your child wishes to dress changed your relationship? Do you force your child to dress a certain way (outside of ensuring reasonable modesty)?

* **People, friends, peers**

Do you approve of his choice in friends, or whom he dates (if he's at dating age)? Do you stop speaking to him if he dates the wrong person, or berate him for the "crowd" he likes to hang out with? How do you respond to his friends? Is it a positive way of dealing with the issue, or are you negative and accusing?

✶ Participation in sports or other school activities

Do you expect him to participate in a sport he barely tolerates, because you believe it's good for him, or because you did it when you were in high school? Could it really be a demand you place on your child so that you have something to do on Friday night, or because your family or friends expect it?

✶ Religious activities

Are you training your older teenager to begin to make his own spiritual decisions, or are you requiring him to participate in every church activity you see fit? Remember, the church drop-out rate after high school is very high. Forcing attendance can have the opposite affect on the teen once they can make their own decisions. Keep the longer term (their entire life) in mind, not just their teen years. The goal should be to find ways for them to become comfortable in their decision to attend church or other religious activities, before they have the freedom to just walk away and never come back. Not expecting attendance is not the answer either. There has to be a balance and some incentives built it.

✶ Participation in family vacations and events

Is your teen required to participate in every family outing, reunion, or holiday celebration as you expect, or do they have some freedom to choose without suffering for it? Is he expected to spend every holiday with difficult extended family members?

✶ Not allowing them to make any mistakes

Does your child feel free to make mistakes and learn from them, or is he afraid of doing the wrong thing for fear you will not accept him anymore? Does your child feel he has to be overachieving or perfect?

✳ Attitudes and ideas different from yours

Can you still love your child when they have a lousy attitude? Do you criticize or alienate your child for having ideas or views different from your own?

Performance-Based vs. Performance-Oriented

There is nothing wrong with expecting your child to do well. In fact, your child needs you to help him understand what you reasonably expect from him. The focus in your relationship is not so much about success or failure in these areas, as much as it is about continuing to love your child through his difficulties. I call that a performance-oriented relationship. Your acceptance is not based on his success. Performance-oriented relationships take the focus off performance and helps your child understand they are valued, no matter what they do.

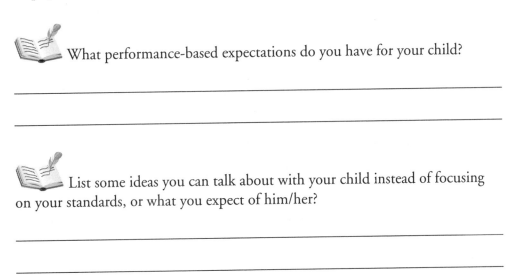 What performance-based expectations do you have for your child?

_____

_____

List some ideas you can talk about with your child instead of focusing on your standards, or what you expect of him/her?

_____

_____

Key Thought

Taking your focus of their performance doesn't mean they never have consequences. It doesn't mean you don't have standards, or expect anything from them. Boundaries and consequences should be applied when you see immaturity, disrespect, deceitfulness, disobedience, or rebellion. In fact, immaturity and defiance demands boundaries and consequences. Neither has anything to do with performance-based acceptance or rejection of your child.

Homework Day Three

When Your Child Fails

The Bible identifies God as a perfect parent. He created two perfect children – Adam and Eve. God gave them a perfect life, the perfect place to live, a perfect job, and a perfect relationship with Him. And yet, Adam and Eve still rebelled and lived imperfect lives. They sinned, and they faced consequences as a result.

Read what happened to them after they sinned:

Look up this scripture: Genesis 3:16–19 (NIV)

"(God) said to the woman, I will greatly increase _____ and your conception; you shall _____, and your desire shall be toward your husband; and he shall rule over you."

And He said to the man, 'Because you have listened to the voice of your wife, and have eaten of the tree about which I commanded you, saying, '_____ _____,' the ground shall be cursed because of you; you shall eat of it in sorrow all the days of your life. And it shall bring forth thorns and thistles for you, and you shall eat the plant of the field. By the sweat of your face you shall eat bread until your return to the ground. For you have been taken out of it; for you are dust, and to dust you shall return."

What were some of the consequences Adam and Eve suffered as a result of their sin? Underline them in the verses above.

Look up this scripture: Genesis 3:21 (NIV)

What did God do for Adam and Eve after they sinned?

"The LORD God made _____ of skin for Adam and his wife and _____ them."

Just imagine! Adam and Eve were two perfect people. But when exercising their free will they made sinful choices. When they sinned they also experienced painful consequences. Even so, God continued to love them with unconditional love, and provided for their needs. Scripture says He covered them. He not only covered them physically, but His actions represented His covering them emotionally and spiritually. Their failure did not change His love for them, not even a little.

Christians do a good job of demanding perfection from one another. The problem with that is that no one is perfect.

Do you feel you need to be a perfect parent, or a perfect spouse? You can't. Do you want your kids to be perfect? They won't be. You will never be perfect. Your child will never be perfect. Christians aren't perfect, just forgiven!

Only God is perfect, and He sees fit to extend grace and mercy to those who aren't. He is the ultimate model of unconditional love.

When your child makes an imperfect choice, he may begin to feel like he can't measure up, or meet the standard set before him by his parents, his church, or his Christian friends. He may feel that he has sinned so profusely that he will never fit in again. Or, he thinks, he has ruined his image with a certain group of people, and can't be around them anymore.

"...we fail when certain standards of behavior, rather than grace and forgiveness, are assumed to be the core of Christianity. In a standards-oriented religion, self-righteousness is for those who appear to be doing what is expected, and for those who aren't adept at deceiving others, the outcome of standards-driven Christianity will be shame." --Dan Allender

Has your child been eliminated from a church group because of his struggles, or making poor choices?

Example: My son was caught smoking at school, dyed his hair black and pierced his lip. His youth leader told him not to come to Youth Group looking and acting that way.

_____

_____

How can you show unconditional love to your child when his character fails?

_____

_____

How has your child been shamed, eliminated, or left out because he doesn't meet a certain "standard?"

_____

_____

Key Thought

Teens are wired to be selfish, untrustworthy, and are prone to make mistakes. The most God-like response to that side of your child's character is to continue to love them unconditionally, even when their attitudes and behavior aren't worthy of it. Again, to be clear, loving them doesn't mean letting them get away with bad behavior without applying appropriate consequences, but be assured, they will make mistakes and that is no reflection on your abilities as a parent.

Homework Day Four

Providing A Way of Restoration

Does your child know there is a path back to you, even when they have walked away from every good thing you taught him?

Christian parents do well to instruct their children to become wise and intelligent; and have their understanding cultivated and improved. Sound discipline is of great worth. A well-disciplined child is far less likely to be tossed around by the self-interests that abound in this culture. It's good to set boundaries around immaturity, and enforce the consequences of defiance, within the context of preserving your relationship.

But what does your relationship become when your child blows it?

Offering Grace

Everyone makes mistakes. We all sin. When your child sins or makes a mistake, it's an opportunity for you to establish grace in your parenting – the same grace God offers you when you sin. God doesn't overlook it, be He does offer a way to maintain a relationship in the midst of it, even when consequences are applied.

Definition of "Grace"

Grace is giving something they don't deserve.

Even when he doesn't deserve it, give grace. Grace isn't enabling. Grace isn't a license to sin. When you give grace, consequences still need to be enforced. And, if a child continues in making poor choices, you can still apply grace, and apply more consequences, and still love him unconditionally.

For example:
You can still take away the car keys as a consequence, but spend time talking with him and express your sorrow in his loss of the keys as you drive him where he needs to go. You can still treat him respectfully and with empathy, even if he

treats you disrespectfully. Yes, you can still stop paying for things if he abuses a privilege, but don't shun him or shame him.

 Write your own example of how you will apply consequences, while at the same time offer grace.

Example: My son revealed today that he is using drugs and drinking while away at college. My response is to stop paying for his college tuition until he stops drinking and using drugs, and let him know I am willing to help him find a counselor in order to deal with his problem. I will require regular, supervised drug or alcohol testing (by the way, testing kits are available from your local pharmacy and there independent drug testing centers in almost every city) as a condition for continued support.

_____

_____

Offering Forgiveness

Look up this scripture: Colossians 3:12-13 (NIV)

"Therefore, as God's chosen people, holy and dearly loved, clothe yourselves with compassion, kindness, humility, gentleness and patience. Bear with each other and _____ you may have against one another. _____ as the Lord forgave you."

In the above scripture, underline how we are to behave toward a child (or anyone) who has sinned.

Write down your behavior toward your child the last time he made a bad decision or a poor choice:

_____

_____

How does your behavior toward your child compare to the characteristics you underlined from Colossians 3?

_____

_____

A counselor's definition of "Forgiveness":
Forgiveness is giving up the hope that you'll ever have a better past.

Name an area your child may need your forgiveness:

_____

_____

Describe how you might go about offering forgiveness:

_____

_____

Offering Mercy

Our definition of "Mercy"
Mercy is NOT getting what you deserve.

A merciful parent tries to understand a child's struggle and help them find a way out of it. Giving your child mercy allows your child a way of escape, not from consequences, but from giving up his relationship with you because of his mistake.

Offering mercy affirms your child in the relationship, even though he messed up. Merciful attitudes point your child back to God and His love, His grace, and His mercy.

Think of a way to give your child a mercy, or something he doesn't deserve this week.

Does your child know the path back toward you is open, even when they've walked away from you? How have you expressed that?

_____

_____

Discuss ways that you can begin to allow more forgiveness, grace and mercy when dealing with your child's struggles or mistakes:

_____

_____

Key Thought

Grace gives a second or third chance. Mercy allows your relationship with your child to continue, even when you are unhappy with their behavior.

Homework Day Five

When Expectations Become Alienation

It's important to find the right balance between expecting too much and expecting too little from your child.

It's not what you expect, it's what you project!

If you project to your child that he mustn't fail, he will start to believe that he can never measure up. Or, if you never acknowledge his successes, he'll give up in frustration. When we expect too much we cause:

* Disappointment
* Discouragement
* Despair
* Despondency

When we expect too little we cause:

* Frustration
* Failure
* Futility

A parent's attitude toward a child is worn on his sleeve like a flashing sign. Just as posting a speed limit sign doesn't keep everyone who drives a car from speeding, your attitude toward your child may or may not make a difference in his choices or decisions.

Instead of expecting too much, and causing overwhelming discouragement, or expecting too little and causing frustration or failure, take a more balanced approach.

Remember, the goal of maintaining a balanced relationship with your child is to have a platform for you to speak both grace and truth into their life at a time of difficulty or struggle.

What area of Grace does your child need from you this week?

_____

_____

 What Truth does your child need to hear from you this week?

_____

_____

 Key Thought

Remember, God is the only perfect parent and even His kids made bad decisions because all of us have a free will. Don't expect perfection, don't project that you are perfect, and don't project that they need to be perfect.

HAVE YOU SEEN
the effects of this confusing culture on your teen?

DO YOU EVER WONDER
if today's teen culture will affect your child?

ARE YOU CONFUSED
trying to navigate in these waters called adolescence?

Teen expert Mark Gregston answers 32 of the toughest questions asked by today's parents concerning their teen, and gives solid insight and practical wisdom on how to approach your teen during the time of their life that they need you the most. Mark shares stories of more than 2,000 teens that have lived with him, and the lessons that he has learned from his involvement in their lives. Whether you have a teen who is struggling, are fearful that your teen might struggle when they enter the teen years, or just want to prepare now for those often turbulent years, this book is for you.

"Mark has a clear, 'big picture' grasp of effective parenting. It's formatted by the power of God's grace and seasoned from decades of experience."

–DR. TIM KIMMEL, President, Family Matters

To purchase this book, visit heartlightresources.org or your local bookstore.

Understanding the Purpose of Pain

My Lesson Notes
Understanding the Purpose of Pain

(Fill in the blanks as underlined items show up on the video screen)

Pain is God's megaphone to a deaf world. --C. S. Lewis

Pain is God's _____ to _____ who we are, _____ how life really is, and brings us to a junction where we seek Him for _____.

God may be using your child to _____ you something as well, _____ and pain is always a precursor to change.

As God never _____ us, we will never _____ our kids.

Foolishness leads to more _____. Wisdom leads to more _____.

"Foolishness" is that determined conviction that happiness must be gained _____ _____ _____ _____ without _____ _____ on God.

"Wisdom" is knowledge of _____ _____ _____ _____ that's gained through observation, reflection and experience.

Pain comes…when there is confrontation for _____ _____.

Pain comes…when they don't _____ with you.

Pain comes…when _____ get heated.

Pain comes…when the _____ of the goal-keeper is established or reestablished.

Pain comes…when the wrong _____, demeanors or _____ are exposed.

_____ doesn't change the pain.

_____ or avoiding your child will not change the pain.

Walking away from a _____ with a rebellious child is not an option.

Compromising your _____ is foolish parenting.

If we _____ our teen, or lessen consequences, the immaturity will continue.

Foolish behavior will always get _____ when _____ _____.

Facing the pain…brings _____.

Facing the _____…brings significance.

_____ is essential in the life of your child to bring about _____ _____ and _____.

©Copyright 2008. May not be copied without permission from the publisher. All rights reserved.

Help is just a phone call away

Family Crisis Coaching from Heartlight offers a voice of hope, and is a place to turn when you're seeking direction for dealing with a struggling, rebellious or distant teen.

every day, hundreds of parents search for help for their teenager's problems. Many don't know what to do or where to turn when their family is turned upside down by a rebellious or self-destructive teen.

Family Crisis Coaching offers help to families caught in these situations. Our coaches are experts in dealing with teens who are out of control and they'll help you defuse the situation and bring sanity back to your home.

This service is a pre-counseling solution for parents. We'll make sure you get started on the right footing with a local counselor, if further help is needed.

Family Crisis Coaching also offers placement advice and assistance for those who may be considering placing their teen in a program outside of the home. Our coaches will guide you in making those decisions if the situation warrants it.

Most of all, you'll gain peace of mind and renewed hope, knowing our coaches have successfully dealt with situations just like yours, again and again. They'll be able to discern whether the behavior you're experiencing can be dealt with through new parenting tactics, or if it is dire enough to demand immediate professional attention.

FAMILY CRISIS COACHING

1-866-700-FAMILY (3264)
903-668-2173

Understanding the Purpose of Pain

THIS WEEK'S FOCUS:

When you stop rescuing your child, and allow him to experience the pain from his actions, it will cause him to think in new ways and learn from his own mistakes.

Homework Day One

Pain – The Precursor to Change

Definition of "Pain":

> *It is the instrument God uses to expose who we really are; explain how life really is, and bring us to a crossroads in life where we will seek Him for answers.*

Pain is a tool that God can use to cause you to question the current circumstances of your life and forces you to reevaluate your goals and motives.

Pain and conflict are precursors to change. Learning to embrace pain properly is what motivates someone to search for a deeper understanding of God's purposes in life.

When we discuss pain, we're generally not talking about physical pain, though putting your finger in a flame will cause you to rethink doing that the next time. We're more talking about the pain of mistreatment from others and the immaturity and irresponsibility that leads to foolish living and painful relationships.

Definition of "Foolishness":

> *The determined conviction that happiness must be gained on my own terms, without significant dependence on God.*

Pain – An Instrument of Change

In parenting, pain is the instrument that God created and uses to help move a person from foolish or dangerous thinking to wisdom. Pain happens in the life of a child through the application of consequences for wrong behavior.

But parents can also act foolish. Instead of allowing their child to experience the consequences of pain, or embracing pain as a useful teaching tool, they rescue or relieve their child of consequences. Rescuing them only allows their teen's foolishness to continue.

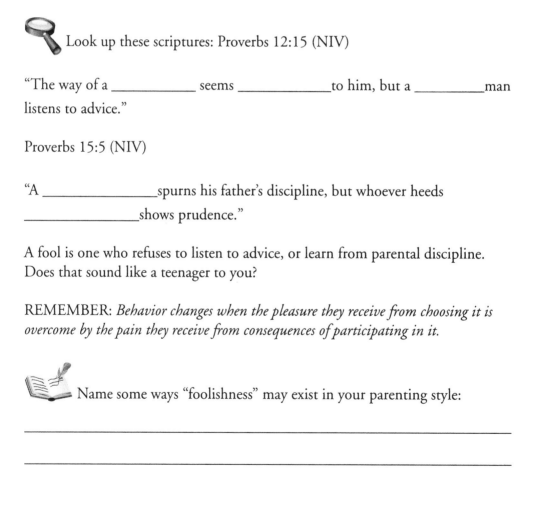 Look up these scriptures: Proverbs 12:15 (NIV)

"The way of a _____ seems _____ to him, but a _____ man listens to advice."

Proverbs 15:5 (NIV)

"A _____ spurns his father's discipline, but whoever heeds _____ shows prudence."

A fool is one who refuses to listen to advice, or learn from parental discipline. Does that sound like a teenager to you?

REMEMBER: *Behavior changes when the pleasure they receive from choosing it is overcome by the pain they receive from consequences of participating in it.*

Name some ways "foolishness" may exist in your parenting style:

_____

_____

 How might you change your approach and address your teen's painful situation according to the biblical model?

Example: In the past I have ignored my son's copying other student's homework in order to allow him to get better grades.

_____

_____

Key Thought

The warning sign of emotional or relational imbalance in the life of a child is pain. Ignoring it only allows the continuation of immaturity – which results in greater pain, and sometimes it becomes a lifelong suffering.

No one likes pain. Parents sometimes get in the way of what God might be trying to do in their child's life by eliminating pain or rescuing their child from the consequences of misbehavior. And parents can short-circuit the positive effect of pain by refusing to engage in the battles where conflict can bring about change.

Homework Day Two

Wisdom Relieves Pain

If pain comes as the result of foolishness, then wisdom is the cure.

Definition of "Wisdom":
The knowledge of the principles of godly living that are gained through observation, reflection, and experience.

Wisdom is gained in one of three ways (O.R.E.):

Observation: What a child sees happening in his life and the life of another.

Reflection: What a child thinks about, ponders, mentally sifts.

Experience: What a child has experienced, both good and bad, in the past.

Wisdom comes into the life of a child through ORE – by way of correction and discipline; in fact, it is the cure for a child's foolish thinking and foolish behavior. Discipline moves them away from foolishness and toward wisdom.

Look up this scripture: Proverbs 19:18 (NIV)

"_____ your son, for in that there is hope; and do not be a willing party to his _____."

What does this scripture say a parent helps a child avoid by properly disciplining him?_____.

What kind of death do you think it means? Is it spiritual death, physical death, or both? Explain your thoughts:

_____

_____

How do your ideas of parenting currently differ from the biblical model?

_____

_____

Homework Day Three

The Nature of Pain

As youngsters we were taught to avoid conflict and walk away from it. We later learned how to appropriately manage conflict in our adult years, when speaking the truth in our relationships became an important way to manage them. The same is true for you and your child.

Confronting pain is a way of moving toward your child, even when they don't want it. It conveys an important message, "I love you enough to stop you from engaging in behavior that will hurt your relationships." It's often just easier to ignore or walk away from a teen's inappropriate behaviors, but better for them in their future relationships if you don't.

Moms spend a lot of time trying to keep their child from feeling lonely, or stupid, or unloved. Dads spend a lot of time trying to prevent a child from feeling helpless, or weak. That's a parent's job, isn't it? But sometimes, confronting their inappropriate behavior or exposing their unlovely behavior is necessary.

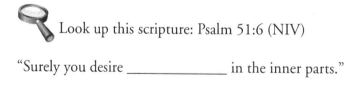 Look up this scripture: Psalm 51:6 (NIV)

"Surely you desire _____ in the inner parts."

Confronting pain means speaking the truth that leads to heartfelt wisdom. It doesn't mean it is easy, but it is a necessary part of disciplining your teen. When you confront pain, be prepared. Pain has a predictable nature, and confronting pain has predictable results.

Pain can appear when:

- ♥ When your values clash with your child's values
- ♥ When you confront their foolish thinking
- ♥ When you and your child have conflicting ideas
- ♥ When you and your child disagree and discussions become "heated"

- ♥ When you establish an area of parental authority, or re-establish your authority
- ♥ When you expose their wrong motives, demeanor, or desires.
- ♥ When your child declares his independence inappropriately
- ♥ When a parent confronts, limits, or restricts a child's wrong thinking.

Rescuing – The Inappropriate Response

Look up this scripture: Proverbs 19:19 (NIV)

"A hot-tempered man must pay the penalty; if you _____ him, you will have to do it again."

What does the Bible call inappropriately keeping a child from experiencing the consequences of his painful attitudes or behavior?

_____

_____

What does the Bible say a parent will have to do if he inappropriately rescues a child from painful attitudes or behavior?

_____

_____

Check the ways you may have rescued your child up to this point:

- ☐ Get busy, don't deal with it, ignore it
- ☐ Over-indulge or try to buy off my child
- ☐ Avoid the problem or pretend it isn't there
- ☐ Walk away from the relationship entirely

- ☐ Compromise standards and accommodate it
- ☐ Develop peace at any cost
- ☐ Bail them out when someone else confronts the problem
- ☐ Don't spend time together anymore
- ☐ Boil, stuff, stew, and allow their issues to destroy my life
- ☐ Worry, instead of confronting their attitudes
- ☐ Laugh it off as teen angst
- ☐ Excuse it as a weakness or medical problem

If you do not properly address pain...

- ✓ Their immaturity will continue
- ✓ Their foolishness and wrong behavior will escalate
- ✓ There will be no pleasure in your life, or your child's
- ✓ You will allow a great misconception about life to continue
- ✓ Your will set your child up for future failure or destruction

Tell of a time when pain appeared at a predictable moment in your child's life.

_____

_____

Describe how you most often handle painful situations with your child right now.

_____

_____

Key Thought

Confronting pain is a process, one that every parent needs to understand and address. How do you feel about being involved in that process – will you continue to protect your child from pain?

Homework Day Four

The Godly Results of Facing Pain - Repentance

Allowing a child to work through their painful behavior brings them recognition that all is not well with the things they have chosen. When your child recognizes his involvement in something that will lead to pain and decides to make a change – this is called repentance.

Definition of "Repentance"
Recognizing false images and beliefs regarding how I meet my personal needs,
And forsaking of them for a commitment to depending on God.

 In the above definition, underline what a repentant attitude recognizes.

 What does our definition say should happen as a result of repentance?

_____

_____

When you confront painful behavior and allow your child to experience the consequences, it:

- ♥ Fosters maturity
- ♥ Helps them develop sensitivity and the ability to recognize pain in others
- ♥ Begins a process of finding the significance they long for
- ♥ Increases their desires and longings for Godly answers
- ♥ Develops an understanding for their need for a Savior.

Don't give in on your position when…

- ♥ You are uncomfortable confronting their behavior, or they don't like it
- ♥ Potential dangers are evident and cannot be ignored

- ♥ Catastrophic consequences are foreseeable
- ♥ Others may be hurt
- ♥ You're being manipulated or disrespected
- ♥ You don't receive support from your spouse, ex-spouse, or others in your family
- ♥ Your values are violated, and you believe they need to be supported
- ♥ When it would be easier to just "give in."

Describe a situation in the past where you "caved in" when you should have held your ground. What was the outcome? Were there long-term effects?

_____

_____

It is good for kids to know that causing pain will lead to consequences. It's important they begin to think for themselves about what is wise and what is foolish. It's not your job to be judgmental or condemning, but to identify consequences. For example, if they speed while driving, they may get an expensive speeding ticket. Let them pay for it. If they cause an accident because of speeding, take away the use of your car.

Develop a discussion with your child about a situation or behavior that is causing pain. Don't offer your advice or find a solution. Instead, just identify the consequences if things don't change. Take time to talk about it over a meal with your child this week. Allow him to come up with a different way to behave all on his own.

Share the outcome with your group (make notes below):

_____

_____

Key Thought

Your role as a parent is to open the door and create a model for your child to learn from pain and its consequences. It's also to help them think through those consequences and come up with better solutions.

Homework Day Five

*"Pain is God's megaphone to a deaf world. I don't doubt God's ability to bless us.
I just wonder how painful it's going to be." – C. S. Lewis*

How God Uses Pain

It's amazing to me that the things I love the most in my wife's character are there as a result of her enduring the pain of childhood sexual abuse. As Jan worked through that pain, God developed in her a wisdom and compassion for others she relies on in our work with struggling teens to this very day. That's not the kind of thing that happened in her life as a result of a poor choice or a bad attitude. But facing it brought her to a new understanding of how God works, and how God doesn't waste pain. God has a purpose for pain, and he promises to use every painful experience in a believer's life for good.

Look up this scripture: Romans 8:28 (NIV)

"And we know that in _____ things God works for the good of those who love Him, who have been called according to _____

_____."

Look up this scripture: Proverbs 4:20 - 27 (NIV)

"My son, _____ to what I say; listen closely to My words. Do not let them out of your sight, keep them within your heart; for they are _____ to those who find them and health to a man's whole body.

Above all else, _____, for it is the wellspring of life. Put away perversity from your mouth; keep corrupt talk far from your lips. Let your eyes look straight ahead, fix your gaze directly before you. Make level paths for your feet and take only ways that are firm. Do not swerve to the right or the left; keep your foot from evil."

In the previous scripture reference, <u>underline</u> how a believer is to handle painful circumstances then (circle) the words that identify what God gives in response to properly addressing pain.

Let Them Draw Their Own Conclusion

You may find it difficult to allow your child to feel the pain of making his own mistakes. Remember our definition from Day One – "Pain is the instrument God uses to bring us to a new understanding of Him, and reveals who we really are, or how life really is. "

Look up this scripture: Proverbs 3:21-24 (NIV)

"My son, preserve _____, do not let them out of your sight; they will be life for you, an ornament to grace your neck. Then you will go on your way in safety, and your foot will not stumble; when you lie down, you will not be afraid; when you lie down, your sleep will be sweet."

According to this passage, what two qualities bring life to the soul?

_____

_____

When a child is allowed to draw some of his own conclusions, it may cause him to think in ways they may never have before. For example; "If I don't have to spend my money on a speeding ticket, I can save it for something special." That's foolish thinking becoming wise.

He may experience a healthy sense of fear about something he wasn't concerned about before, or recognize that he is involved in something that is not good for him. That's discretion.

Think about your child's immaturity, irresponsibility, or painful behaviors.

 What painful behavior or attitude does your child need to confront?

_____

_____

What consequences does your child need to experience?

_____

_____

What new conclusion does your child need to draw for himself?

_____

_____

Key Thought

Drawing his own conclusions may cause your teen to think in ways he never has before. He may experience a healthy sense of fear about something he wasn't concerned about before, or recognize that he is involved in something that is not good for him. That's foolish thinking becoming wise thinking.

Heartlight

RESIDENTIAL COUNSELING CENTER FOR TEENS

For more information about Heartlight, or to receive an admission packet, please call 903.668.2173 or visit our website at www.HeartlightMinistries.org

AN ATMOSPHERE OF

relationships

Nestled among the beautiful piney woods of East Texas, Heartlight Ministries provides a residential counseling setting for adolescents in crisis situations. With a capacity for 48 co-ed residents, Heartlight offers intense, individual attention that fosters an atmosphere of relationships. This interaction with staff, residents and other families provides an arena for change and a chance to gain wisdom, support, and encouragement through difficult times.

When situations of divorce, death, abuse, social difficulties, academic struggles, adoption issues and unhealthy coping mechanisms (lying, selfishness, manipulation, entitlement, depression, lack of motivation, disrespect for authority, confusion) are present, Heartlight offers an answer when removal from the home is necessary. Founded in 1989, the Heartlight program has proven successful in the lives of hundreds of teens and their families.

CREATES AN ARENA FOR change

Developing Boundaries for Your Teen

My Lesson Notes
Developing Boundaries for Your Teen

(Fill in the blanks as underlined items show up on the video screen)

Boundaries _____ family members and your home from being _____.

_____ is probably the greatest issue that has to happen in your home.

To gain respect, a parent needs to be _____ of their teen.

A boundary allows you as a parent to be _____ _____ _____, and creates a zone of comfort.

A boundary says, "We will not _____ _____ _____.

_____ are the necessary parameters set up to support boundaries.

Rules shouldn't exist solely to restrain freedom or take away privileges, but exist to support your _____.

Parents who set boundaries model for their children to say "No" to _____ influences.

Boundaries reinforced by _____ and backed up by _____ _____ helps keep a child moving along the right path.

Consequences serve two purposes. They move a child down the path they need to go. They keep them from going where they _____ _____.

Wisdom comes from….O.R.E. _____ – _____ – Experience.

©Copyright 2008. May not be copied without permission from the publisher. All rights reserved.

Developing Boundaries for Your Teen

THIS WEEK'S FOCUS:

*Boundaries teach your child how to give and receive respect.
Without knowing boundaries, children remain immature.*

Homework Day One

Boundaries Define You

Does your child understand that in life there are limits? Do you want your child to learn to respect you and others? Knowing what you believe, and having a system in place for implementing healthy boundaries teaches your children to respect your beliefs, and helps them successfully transition from the pre-teen era of selfishness and immaturity to an era of self-control more successfully.

Boundaries are those parameters or fences that define your own personal space. They describe what is yours and what is not. A boundary may include locks on your doors, words that reflect your personal desires, or standards, and principles by which you choose to live. Boundaries make distinctions between what is off-limits and what is acceptable behavior.

*A boundary details where you end and someone else begins.
Boundaries lead you to a sense of ownership.*

Boundaries are sometimes confused with rules. Boundaries deal more with the person, and rules deal more with "things" or "methods." Boundaries are not about necessarily how your home will run. Instead, boundaries are definitions about you and your "yard." You are the gate-keeper.

As you begin to think about boundaries, ask yourself, *"What do I want the relationships and behavior in my home to look like?"*

In the following list, check the personal boundaries that identify how you would like to be treated, or have your home operate. <u>Underline</u> the personal boundaries that are problem areas with teens in your home right now (if any).

- ☐ Kindness
- ☐ Yelling
- ☐ Honesty
- ☐ Stealing
- ☐ Obedience
- ☐ Deceit
- ☐ Respect
- ☐ Anger
- ☐ Permissiveness
- ☐ Overbearing behavior
- ☐ My teen's independence

- ☐ Temper tantrums
- ☐ Self-control
- ☐ Maturity
- ☐ Stealing
- ☐ Joy
- ☐ Humility
- ☐ Selfishness
- ☐ Living peacefully
- ☐ Lying
- ☐ Patience

Look up this scripture: Galatians 5:22-23 (NIV)

"But the fruit of the Spirit is love, joy, peace, patience, kindness, goodness, faithfulness, gentleness, and _____-_____. Against such things there is no law."

Rank how your child is doing in the area of self-control. (Circle)

1	2	3	4	5	6	7	8	9	10
Little or No Self-Control				Needs to Learn More			Completely Self-Controlled		

Name one or two specific areas of self-control your child struggles with:

_____

_____

> ### *Examples of Boundaries;*
>
> #### *My Personal Space*
> *I decide who touches me and who doesn't*
>
> #### *My Time*
> *I decide to whom or to what I will give my time...it is not decided by someone else*
>
> #### *My Words*
> *I know how I would like to speak to others, and how I would like others to speak to me*
>
> #### *My Truth*
> *I have freedom to tell the truth instead of hiding behind a falsehood,*
> *I would like others to be truthful with me as well*
>
> #### *My Distance*
> *I choose to be where I go and how long I will be there*
>
> #### *My Emotional Freedom*
> *I am not responsible for what others think, I won't accept my teen "dumping" on me*

Hopefully, this list helps you see how boundaries organize the arena for relationships within your home. They help teach your child how to respect another's time, energy, space, and authority. They ultimately teach your child self-control in many areas.

Personal boundaries are also the number one way to teach your child how to give and receive respect. Without knowing their boundaries, children remain immature, and do not learn respect.

 What are some of your current personal boundaries?

_____

_____

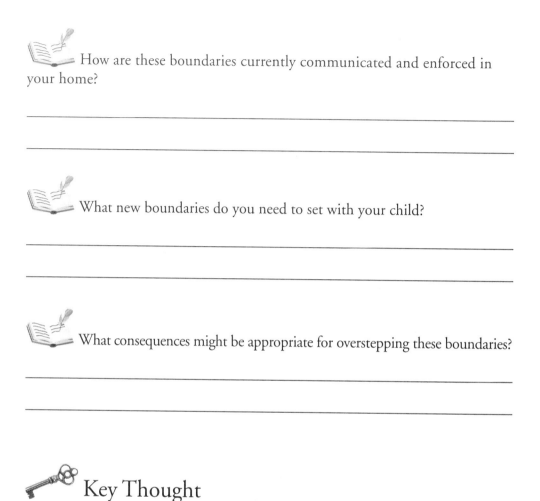

How are these boundaries currently communicated and enforced in your home?

_____

_____

What new boundaries do you need to set with your child?

_____

_____

What consequences might be appropriate for overstepping these boundaries?

_____

_____

Key Thought

Healthy boundaries teach your child the art of self-control and respect for others.

Homework Day Two

Boundaries Shift as a Teen Matures

As parenting moves from providing for a pre-teen child to that of preparing the adolescent to become a mature adult, a shift in boundaries is also required. Some boundaries shift from that which what was once allowed to that which is no longer allowed – like no longer allowing an older child to rummage through your purse. Or, not tolerating immature temper tantrums when your teen doesn't get what he wants.

New boundaries must be established as your teen gets older – like teaching them to knock before entering your bedroom, instead of waltzing in without asking. Or, asking permission before borrowing someone else's things. Or, a boy having a teenage girl in his room with the door closed.

New Boundaries – New Freedoms

If parents set more mature boundaries with forethought, they'll offer them as a gift to the teen, making them feel you trust them more. They'll then enjoy meeting their new responsibility.

But when more strict boundaries and responsibilities are given in the midst of conflict and crisis, then a child feels restricted or limited at a time in their life when they believe they should be given more freedom and greater territory. Instead of changing the boundaries, the consequences are what need to get more severe as the teen continues to break boundaries you've already established.

That's why it's important to determine your boundaries early in your child's life, when they are accustomed to your authority, and make sure you communicate them often. Those boundaries should grow with your child's maturity. Imposing new boundaries on a teen who has never had them before is a disaster waiting to happen, so be sure to take thoughtful steps and give time for the new boundaries to take effect. Don't just spring it on them.

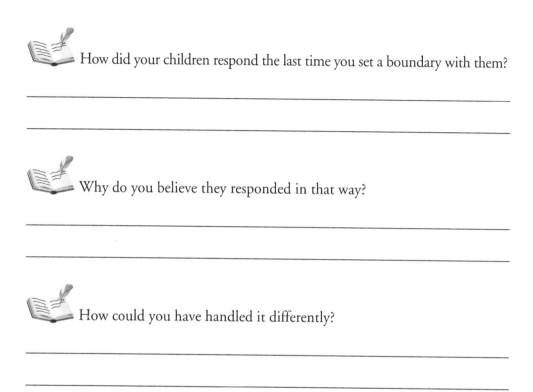

How did your children respond the last time you set a boundary with them?

_____

_____

Why do you believe they responded in that way?

_____

_____

How could you have handled it differently?

_____

_____

It is also important that you continue to shift your boundaries early in their adolescence – before you think they need it. Shifting your boundaries means moving off of controlling their behavior, to teaching them the fruit of self-control. There are times it's best to say to your early adolescent child, "I can't do that with you, I think you'll be fine if you go it alone." And let them go. Too many parents don't make this shift and end up provoking their children, who become frustrated, irritated, and aggravated.

Can you give an example of a time your child showed irritation because you did or said something (or maybe it was even the way you said something) that might have seemed like a throwback to the discipline from their younger years?

_____

_____

If your kids are older, where are you on the parenting pendulum? Are you still deciding everything for them, or preparing them to decide for themselves?

1	2	3	4	5	6	7	8	9	10
Hopelessly Over-Controlling		Still Deciding Most Things		Handing Over Control			Letting Them Take Control		

How might establishing some new personal boundaries help them do more for themselves?

_____

_____

Do you agree that there are times it might be best for your child to act without you alongside to help? Why, or why not?

_____

_____

 Identify a boundary that has shifted as your teen matures. For instance, what in your home was once allowed that is no longer allowed or vice versa?

_____

_____

Key Thought

Boundaries needs to shift in order to move a child from a position of being over-controlled by parents to that of learning the art of self-control.

Homework Day Three

Boundaries Are Reinforced by Rules

Think of boundaries, rules and consequences in this way: Boundaries are the broader ethics like those established in the Ten Commandments. Rules are the laws enacted by society to enforce those Commandments. And consequences are the penalties applied if someone were to break the rules.

For example, we believe in honesty, so we will enact rules and consequences should a child to lie to us. The rule for your home could be: *"I expect everyone to tell me the truth. I will always tell you the truth, even if it is difficult to do so."*

This rule helps your child understand your boundary of honesty. He's not allowed to lie. Since we value honesty so greatly, dishonesty may have more severe consequences than what he's trying to cover up by being untruthful.

If your boundaries include valuing sexual purity before marriage, then your house rules will not allow sexually explicit materials to be viewed in your home. Computers will have filtering software installed, and you will evaluate each movie, magazine, book, or other forms of entertainment in light of that boundary.

If your boundary is that you would like to receive respect, then your rule is, "I would like to be spoken to with respect. Everyone in our home will be treated respectfully. I will respect you. When away from home, we will treat others with respect."

Definition of a "Rule"
Rules are the practical application of broader boundaries.
Rules are determined by what I believe to be true (my faith),
and are designed to develop character in my child.

What Rules are Not

- ♥ Rules are not to make you feel better about your parenting or to make your parenting easier. They are for your child's benefit and training.
- ♥ Rules are not meant to browbeat a child into submission.
- ♥ Rules are not rigid. They change over time and are appropriate to age.
- ♥ Rules are not Consequences. Consequences are the enforcement of rules.
- ♥ Rules are not intended to punish, shame, or make your child feel badly about himself.
- ♥ Rules are not set in concrete. As your boundaries shift, so must your rules.

As you begin to enforce rules, your child will feel freedom in knowing what's expected. They'll learn a sense of self-control from following the rules, and a sense of personal confidence that says, "I know the right path to take through this yard."

What are some of your current house rules?

_____

_____

As you think about your personal boundaries, how do your house rules tend to support them?

_____

_____

What current rules need to be shifted to accommodate for your teen's growing level of maturity and to allow them room to make mistakes?

_____

_____

 Key Thought

As you begin to enforce rules, your child will feel freedom in knowing what's expected. They'll learn a sense of self-control from following the rules, and gains a sense of personal confidence that says, "I know the right path to take through this yard."

Homework Day Four

Boundaries Direct Your Child's Path

Just as God directs your path, it is your job to initially direct your teen's path. When parents are strong in setting personal boundaries, it models for a child how to set boundaries of their own. What better way to teach your child the way to say "no" to evil influences than to train him in setting right boundaries for himself?

Boundaries also direct your teen's path by letting him know what to expect, all along life's way. The reward in establishing healthy boundaries becomes obvious in their adulthood. Directing them along right paths today helps them with choices they make as adults; in who they marry, how they treat their spouse, their children, their employer and their neighbor.

Remember, the intent of a boundary is always to help your child learn something important, like respecting others, finishing a job they start, spending their time more wisely, or offering help to someone when they need it. It puts them into the place of deciding to comply with those in authority, or not.

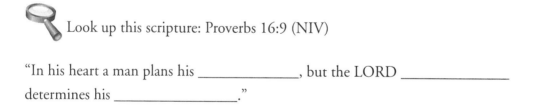 Look up this scripture: Proverbs 16:9 (NIV)

"In his heart a man plans his _____, but the LORD _____ determines his _____."

On a scale of one to ten, (ten being great) how do you feel you are doing in preparing your child to leave home and function in the world in a healthy way? Explain.

(circle)

1   2   3   4   5   6   7   8   9   10

One of the greatest threats to your personal and family boundaries is the busyness of life and the demands of numerous activities. Mom or Dad's role as parent and family authority begin to play "second fiddle" to the roles of taxi driver, school project manager, study hall monitor, and money-tree keeper. It's difficult to honor family boundaries and enforce the rules when everyone is so busy.

 How has the barrenness of busyness affected your ability to set boundaries for you and your family? Have you sometimes overlooked enforcing or teaching boundaries out of lack of time or energy?

Look up this scripture: Hebrews 13:5 (NIV)

"Keep your lives free from the love of money and be content with what you have, because God has said, 'Never will I leave you; never will I forsake you.'"

How does this principle of contentedness affect your ideas about your family schedule and boundaries?

_____

_____

Do you feel your child is on the right path in life, or has he/she fallen off track?

_____

_____

Given enough time, how might setting up a new boundary change the direction or path he/she is currently on?

_____

_____

Key Thought

Your child may never fully agree with any of your boundaries, but he or she can be required to respect your boundaries, even if they don't agree with them.

Homework Day Five

Consequences

Today's lesson is more of a warning than anything else. Just as there are some horses that cannot be broken, there are some teens who won't respond well to having new boundaries placed into their life.

When a teen has to learn about honoring someone's boundaries the hard way they go through adolescence clueless about respect, honesty, and obedience, They stumble off to college, to work, or to become parents themselves leaving in their wake a path of destructive behavior and relational missteps.

> *Teens suffer a lot of unnecessary consequences for a parent's lack of training about boundaries, rules, and consequences.*

The lack of boundaries can cause a teen to be angry. They are unprepared to meet the demands of their world with the confidence to say, "Here is where I begin and end. This is me, and that is not me. This is who I am and where I will draw the line."

Sometimes parents need to turn their child over to the consequences of their choices. How does that differ from giving up on a child?

_____

_____

A failure to enforce rules with consequences allows your child to ignore your boundaries, and function in a mode that has no respect for you or others. Which of your boundaries does your child currently ignore?

Example: My teen speaks to me disrespectfully when I won't let him use my car.

_____

_____

 How might enforcing a new or different consequence change his behavior or attitude?

_____

_____

Key Thought

Parents who refuse to enforce healthy boundaries at home set a teen up for a life of learning about boundaries the hard way.

Developing a Belief System for Discipline

My Lesson Notes
Developing a Belief System for Discipline

(Fill in the blanks as underlined items show up on the video screen)

A _____ System…Helping your family move in a _____ direction.

Beliefs are dearly held _____, opinions, ideals, morals.

Rules are _____ that _____ your beliefs, and determine what is acceptable and unacceptable.

Consequences are _____ _____ _____ a child in a new direction and are not just for punishment.

Your child will continue in the same actions until the _____ from those actions is greater than the _____ they derive from it.

Address the _____ most important areas of change.

Belief System Example #1

Belief…

Mom and Dad would like to be spoken to with _____.

Family members are to be respectful to _____ _____.

Rule…

Talk with _____ to siblings, parents and others.

Consequence

Minor Infraction: Loss of _____ _____ .

Appropriate consequences: Take away something they _____ for a time, including privileges and freedoms.

The recurring rule breaker....._____ _____ of privileges or freedoms.

Major Infraction: Loss of a _____ privilege.

Belief System Example #2

Belief...

We believe it is unhealthy for a teen to smoke cigarettes, drink alcohol or to use illegal drugs.

Rule...

No underage _____ , no _____ , no _____ .

A parent may need to engage in _____ systems to ensure rules are not being broken.

Consequence

Minor Infraction: _____ for one month.

Major Infraction: Loss of _____ privileges, for a _____ period.

Belief System Example #3

Belief…

Some entertainment choices can be harmful.

Rule…

Movies of certain ratings must be _____ in advance. Same applies for video games, online entertainment and television.

Music with profane language, or violent or sexual overtones is subject to _____ and approval.

Consequence

Minor Infraction: Loss of the _____ _____ for a time.

Major Infraction: Loss of the offending item for a _____ period of time.

Major or Repeated Infraction: _____ ____! (remove the offending item).

Step One

Develop a list of _____ important areas of change for your family.

Step Two

Call a family _____.

Step Three

Share your concerns and reasons for wanting a _____.

Step Four

Meet again to discuss _____ and _____.

Step Five

Discuss _____, rules and consequences and ask for _____.

Step Six

_____ beliefs, rules and consequences and announce when they will

_____.

Step Seven

_____ through!

Step Eight

Review every _____ _____. Adjust to make sure rules and

consequences are _____ – _____.

Message to your child…"There will be _____ in our home."

2nd Message to your child…"We won't allow _____ _____ to

continue."

Notes _____

_____

_____

_____

©Copyright 2008. May not be copied without permission from the publisher. All rights reserved.

Developing a Belief System for Discipline

> ### LEARN MORE...
>
> *More about developing a Belief System for your home, including worksheets and examples, can be found at the end of this workbook on page 168.*

Homework Day One

Your Beliefs Structure Your Discipline

Every parent longs for the relationships in their home to be healthy, peaceful, and beneficial to one another. One of the most helpful things you can do to build healthy family relationships before your child reaches the teen years is to create a roadmap for how your home and family will operate. You may ask, "Why do my beliefs matter? You can't argue with what someone believes, can you? After all, what you believe is important is unique. What you believe is probably the most appropriate thing for your family. Your teen might not agree, but it doesn't matter, this is what you believe should happen, and this is what you will work to make happen.

> *Your Belief System for Discipline is a clearly defined determination of how the relationships in your home function, and is reinforced with rules and consequences – based upon your beliefs.*

Implementing a system of discipline, and fostering a change in the way things are around your house may be more difficult than you realize – especially when you've never really functioned that way before. But, it's not impossible. It's a time consuming process, but a worthwhile investment. It's never too late to share with your child your longing for better relationships within your family, or that you believe relationships do best when everyone knows what to expect.

Identifying What Needs to Change

Begin right now to think about what you want to be different, and start to write those things down. Would you like to have more respect? Would you like your teen to have better time management? Who pays for their telephone, gas, or insurance? Would you like everyone to stop yelling, and start listening? What takes priority, driving to work or driving elsewhere?

Parents with out-of-control kids manage their child's problems on a day-to-day basis. They don't take time to set up a system of rules and consequences, much less communicate them to their child. If you want to implement change and avoid family chaos, start today by thinking about what you long for, and what you believe. After all, your home is the primary place your child will learn what you believe, and ultimately what they believe.

Where do most of your beliefs about parenting come from? Are they biblical, familial, or cultural?

_____

_____

Share with the class something you used to believe that doesn't really apply anymore. "When I'm a parent, I will never..." Example: *I will never feed my child candy, since it will rot his teeth.*

_____

_____

 How difficult do you think it will be for your family to operate under a Belief System? Where would be the most helpful place start? How can others in your class help you?

_____

_____

 Key Thought

Relationships flourish when everyone knows what to expect.

Homework Day Two

Step 1: Determining Your Beliefs

Definition of a "Belief"
*A conviction, opinion, ideal, value, or moral held because of
your faith, past experience, family tradition, culture, or marriage.*

If I asked you to name the top ten most important things about your family relationships, what would you write down? Where do your beliefs come from? Are they based in your faith? Do they come from your own past? Do they reflect the ideas of modern culture? Do they come from your social circle? What do you believe are the most important character qualities you want to see in your child?

To help you get started, let me offer a few examples:

Begin with three very important character qualities every parent wants to develop in their child; Respect, Honesty, and Obedience. Developing respect is at the top of your list. As we learned in another lesson, without respect, there is no foundation for a relationship. Perhaps you also value safety, modesty, and taking responsibility for myself. And maybe you believe the Bible calls you to honor God, honor others, be helpful, and be spiritually ready to meet your Maker in heaven. Those may be your top ten.

So, begin to make a list, without setting down any rules or consequences yet. Examine what you hold dear, and why it is important to you. You may find that some of the beliefs you grew up with are valuable to you, and some of them are not. Some of your beliefs may be totally unreasonable, totally useless, or totally ridiculous, and need to be replaced with better beliefs or values. Start with a list of ten, and go from there.

What are the ten most important beliefs about the way my home should operate?

1. Respect (we'll help on this one, just in case you weren't sure where to start!)

2. _____

3. _____

4. _____

5. _____

6. _____

7. _____

8. _____

9. _____

10. _____

Circle two or three of your beliefs you value the most, and would like to begin to work on immediately. Underline new thoughts or ideas, and ask for feedback from your class – perhaps others also believe the same thing!

Key Thought

Respect is the cornerstone for building good relationships.

Homework Day Three

Creating Rules

Definition of "Rules"
Rules are parameters established to enforce the Belief System for your home.

Once you have a grasp on your top ten beliefs (remember, you can add more as your understanding of what you truly believe develops) then create some rules to help reinforce those beliefs.

Try to make the strategy for enforcing the rules "fit" your family's needs, keeping in mind that what worked for your family when your children were younger will most likely need to be updated for when your children become teens. Outmoded or outdated rules fail every time. Keep things current and relevant to the process.

As an example; if you believe in honesty, you will tell your children the truth. And you will expect your children to tell the truth. You are honest in your dealings with others. You won't support your child cheating on a test, copying another's homework, or being deceitful. The house rule is this: <u>Everyone is to be honest, even if it is painful to do so or results in negative consequences</u>.

Another example is this; you believe in respect. Therefore, everyone in your home will be respected, on many levels. The rules are: we will speak and act respectfully toward one another, we will treat those outside our family with respect, and we will respect one another's time, space, and energy.

Here's another. If you believe in spiritual training your rules could be: our family attends church on a regular basis, and we will spend one week on a mission project each summer.

Do you see how what you believe becomes the cornerstone for the rules that govern your home? Rules support your beliefs, and train your child. They ultimately develop character. They are not only intended to limit freedom, or punish, but to protect and train your child to make good decisions.

 Assignment: Think of a rule for each of the beliefs you listed in Day Two. Ask your class members or discussion leader for help, if you need to.

Key Thought

If you are not sure if your rules are reasonable, too strict, or too lax, ask for help. Some of your rules may need to be adjusted.

Homework Day Four

Definition of "Consequences"
The results brought on by breaking the rules – primarily designed to establish the path parents would like to have their child walk, and not just a way to punish negative behavior.

Consequences, more than anything else, keep your child from choosing to behave in a way that is out of line with what you believe, or for breaking a rule. Consequences are not solely punishment for doing wrong. (However, punishment may become a part of their consequences, depending upon the severity of the infraction – especially if others are put in danger or hurt in the process).

Consequences at this stage of a teen's life should bring about:

Correction, Direction, and Guidance,

and are not meant to be

Punishment, Vengeance, or Retribution.

Consequences direct your child's path when he is headed the wrong way by limiting his ability to continue to move in that direction. They keep your teenager's life from going to a place in life they really do not want to go.

Remember, the consequences reinforce rules, and what you believe, and should "fit" your family's current needs and be age-appropriate.

Some examples of consequences include the loss of participation in certain enjoyed activities or time with friends, the loss of privileges, and the loss of anything plugged in or has batteries (like an Ipod, computer, stereo, gaming device, cell phone) or a requirement for extra work. Teens need to be reminded that the freedoms and material things they enjoy are privileges, not rights.

Examples:

Here are some basic belief/rule/consequence scenarios that may be helpful to you in thinking through your own belief system:

Academics
* **Belief:** We believe that our children (unless they are somehow mentally challenged) should bring home passing grades throughout high school.
* **Rule:** There will be no failing grades in high school.
* **Consequences:** No car privileges until all grades are passing (one example of many potential consequences).

Spiritual
* **Belief:** We believe it is important to be spiritually trained and receive regular spiritual input.
* **Rule:** Our family attends church at least once weekly, and spends time every summer on a mission project.
* **Consequence:** Loss of Friday night out if they miss church that week. Pay for skateboard camp when they complete their mission project. (Consequences can be positive too!)

Social
* **Belief:** We believe that nothing good happens to teens away from home after midnight
* **Rule:** Curfew is midnight on weekends. Curfew is 9 p.m. on school nights. (Remember, this is an example, not a recommendation!)
* **Consequence:** Curfew violation results in loss of allowance for two weeks. (I know of one parent who made their teen pay $1 per minute for every minute they came in late!) Reward them for honoring curfew with occasional "time off" from some other duty or chore.

Behavioral
* **Belief:** We believe that every family member and their belongings should be treated with respect.
* **Rule:** All family members will treat everyone with the utmost respect.

* **Consequence:** First infraction: grounding for one week (no privileges except school attendance and job responsibilities). If disrespect continues, grounding for two weeks with the loss of car, loss of allowance. If this is not effective, the car is sold or the computer is given away. If 18 or over, a discussion about what it takes to continue living at home.

Character:
* **Belief:** Everyone should be challenged to improve their character.
* **Rule:** Each child will meet with mom or dad for breakfast one morning a week to discuss life, issues, ideas, and the future. If character is a problem, a meeting with a counselor might be added.
* **Consequence:** If a child misses, their Friday or Saturday night out is cancelled as well. If mom or dad misses – you owe your child $50.

Medical:
* **Belief:** We believe every family member should follow qualified medical advice.
* **Rule:** Prescribed treatments are to be followed.
* **Consequence:** If medicine is not taken, there will be no use of IPODS, TV, or other electronics.

Possessions
* **Belief:** We believe that rooms should be cleaned at least once a week.
* **Rule:** Each family member's room can be messy if they want, but rooms must be tidied up weekly and deep-cleaned every month. Cleaning means dusting, vacuuming, cleaning all surfaces, and the ability to see the floor.
* **Consequence:** Loss of allowance until room is cleaned. Loss of car for weekend, loss of car for a month.

Entertainment:
* **Belief:** Mom and Dad believe that entertainment should be wholesome.
* **Rule:** Anything but G-rated movies must be approved by a parent, and they must be reviewed a few days in advance. Music that glorifies death, violence, profanity, or sex will not be allowed.
* **Consequence:** Loss of that entertainment, TV or Stereo for a week, two weeks, or a month.

Responsibilities:
* **Belief:** A child should be able to do their laundry after age 12
* **Rule:** Each person does his own laundry: wash, fold and put away every week.
* **Consequence:** If laundry isn't done, soiled clothes are captured by the Laundry Queen (Mom) and can be purchased back from her. Or, laundry may be gathered and taken to the cleaners, where they can pay to get them back.

Privileges:
* **Belief:** Mom and Dad believe that it is safer when they know where everyone is when away from home.
* **Rules:** We are to know where you are. When a change of plan happens, call to get permission before you go.
* **Consequence:** Failure to notify a parent of changes will result in a four-hour work-project that must be completed right away, even if they have to give up other plans in order to do so. Loss of cell phone for a week. Loss of car use for two weeks.

Family
* **Belief:** Mom and Dad believe that everyone's busy schedules undermine family unity, and that the family needs to spend at least one night a week together.
* **Rule:** Monday night is the designated Family Night, beginning with dinner at 6 p.m. and doing something together afterwards.
* **Consequence:** No inheritance (well, not really).

As you can see, humor can soften the blow a little, and make the consequences more palatable. Most teens would look at this list and feel "put-out." But it's an example of a good place to start. "Big issues" with kids are disrespect, disobedience, and dishonesty. These should therefore bring heavy consequences. Inappropriate behavior at the top of any list would include drug or alcohol use, driving under the influence, and issues surrounding violence or sex.

What area of change will be difficult for me to enforce healthy consequences?

_____

_____

Check the three things your child most values, and would hate to lose as a result of breaking a rule:

☐ Cell phone
☐ Ipod
☐ Computer/games
☐ Internet access
☐ Gas
☐ Insurance
☐ Using the car
☐ Time with friends
☐ Time with other family
☐ Trips
☐ Spa/salon visit
☐ Shopping trip
☐ Money/allowance

☐ Time for sports
☐ College tuition fund
☐ Something you loan him/her
☐ Youth group events
☐ Rides to school
☐ CD's
☐ Television
☐ Private bedroom
☐ Name your own:

_____

☐ Name your own:

_____

Rank Your Current Level of Enforcing Consequences:

☐ Non-Existent
☐ Softie
☐ Door Mat
☐ Well-Balanced
☐ Drill Sergeant
☐ Controlling
☐ Abuser

Rank Your <u>Spouse's</u> Current Level of Enforcing Consequences:

- ☐ Non-Existent
- ☐ Softie
- ☐ Door Mat
- ☐ Well-Balanced
- ☐ Drill Sergeant
- ☐ Controlling
- ☐ Abuser

Reminder...
Go to page 168 for a more comprehensive discussion of Belief Systems, including worksheets.

 Key Thought

It helps to think about your top priorities, and what your child values most. Take away their most valued possession or privilege for a time for breaking your most important belief, like respect in the home. Lesser penalties can be applied to lesser important beliefs.

Homework Day Five

Implementing Change

If you are a parent who has trouble with enforcing consequences for fear of your child's reaction, you have a choice to make – continue to live in fear of your child or learn how to enforce consequences. It's the most important thing a parent can do to change the direction of a child's thinking.

You can correct their attitudes and behavior now, or allow them to get worse. Your child may be unhappy, get angry with you, pout, yell, scream, or even get physical and abusive. Such a response only proves the need for implementing change within your family.

Families who are not strong in the "relationship" department need time to adjust to a new way of operating. It helps if your child understands your motivation. Explain to your family before you hand out the rules and decide on the consequences that you have a longing in your heart to build better relationships. In order for that to happen, you will all have to work hard to build up the relationship side of your family by spending more time together.

Implementing change is best done by calling a series of family meetings. Introduce your concerns, but don't try to solve every problem all at once. Use the family meeting times to identify an area and to work on creating rules, and consequences.

First Meeting: "I'm not happy with some ways our family has been operating. I long for our family to have better relationships. I believe our family is worth making things better." Don't share specifics – just ask everyone to think about it, and schedule the next meeting.

Next meeting: Identify some areas of change, without revealing what you will do about them. "I don't think we spend enough time together building our family relationships. I'm too busy at work. You are too busy with sports, or lessons, or activities."

"I want to see us treat one another with more respect."

"I don't like how we're taking care of the house right now."

Don't problem-solve at this meeting, simply ask for their input, and schedule the next meeting.

Third Meeting: Be a little more specific, and set down some rules:

"I believe we need to be more respectful to one another. I promise to respect you, and you will be expected to respect me. The rule for our family is; we will treat each other with respect, at all times. When away from our home, we will treat others with respect."

Don't mention consequences yet, just let your child mentally adapt, and make sure they understand the rule before the meeting ends. Ask them to think about what the consequences should be for breaking the rule, and bring them to the next meeting.

Final Meeting: Talk about the rules and identify the consequences. Let your family help you develop the right consequences, and make them age-appropriate. You'll be surprised that your teens will come up with more severe consequences than you do. Choose a date down the road for the rules and consequences to kick in.

If your child is unhappy about having new limits, remain dedicated to enforcing them. "We will be respectful to one another. It begins tomorrow."

Consequences rarely fail when they are relevant and enforced. Managing consequences is one of the most important roles a parent fulfills.

 How have you failed to apply appropriate consequences in the past? What was the result?

_____

_____

Write down an area where you are "stuck" when it comes to consequences, and ask your group for helpful ideas to get unstuck.

_____

_____

_____

_____

Key Thought

Every child wants and needs to know how to take control of their lives. They want structure, and desire to know your boundaries. Just a little discipline and structure can go a long way toward helping a child move along the right path.

Help is just a phone call away

Family Crisis Coaching from Heartlight offers a voice of hope, and is a place to turn when you're seeking direction for dealing with a struggling, rebellious or distant teen.

every day, hundreds of parents search for help for their teenager's problems. Many don't know what to do or where to turn when their family is turned upside down by a rebellious or self-destructive teen.

Family Crisis Coaching offers help to families caught in these situations. Our coaches are experts in dealing with teens who are out of control and they'll help you defuse the situation and bring sanity back to your home.

This service is a pre-counseling solution for parents. We'll make sure you get started on the right footing with a local counselor, if further help is needed.

Family Crisis Coaching also offers placement advice and assistance for those who may be considering placing their teen in a program outside of the home. Our coaches will guide you in making those decisions if the situation warrants it.

Most of all, you'll gain peace of mind and renewed hope, knowing our coaches have successfully dealt with situations just like yours, again and again. They'll be able to discern whether the behavior you're experiencing can be dealt with through new parenting tactics, or if it is dire enough to demand immediate professional attention.

FAMILY CRISIS COACHING
1-866-700-FAMILY (3264)
903-668-2173

LESSON 8

Issues of Control

My Lesson Notes
Issues of Control

(Fill in the blanks as underlined items show up on the video screen)

Your job as a parent is to make sure your child has _____

_____ of their life at the end of adolescence.

Who's in _____ of your home?

Is your control over your home based more on your own needs or the needs of your _____?

Allow your kids to move on to the _____ step in life.

Allow them _____. Through mistakes they will learn to make better decisions.

Over-control: When a parent sets overly _____ _____ and sets too many limits.

"_____ children are subject to dependency, enmeshment conflict, and have difficulty setting and keeping firm boundaries. They also have problems taking risks and being creative." Dr. Henry Cloud –*Boundaries.*

Under-control: Lack of good _____.

_____ produces a child who is selfish, independent, demanding and aggressively controlling.

Under-control is often seen in divorce settings or when parents try to act like _____.

Moms tend to keep control _____ _____. Dads tend to give it up ____ ____ _____.

Spend more time in discussion and less time _____.

Lead with _____.

Invite them to begin making _____ for themselves.

Start allowing children to exercise making their own choices at age _____ or _____

Ask for their _____ or their viewpoint.

Questions offer a sense of _____ to your child's opinion.

Don't share your opinions unless they _____ _____ ___.

Help your child say, "_____," and honor it.

It's okay, and even healthy, to have respectful _____ of opinion.

Model humility, admit when you are _____.

"Solid food is for the mature, who, because of _____…have their senses trained to discern between good and evil." – Hebrews 5:14

Learn to have _____.

A discussion needs to be a _____ – way street.

"Responsibility" is being _____ or _____ to, accountable for, or to be answerable to. The ability to be accountable to someone else for activities involving obligations or duties.

"Maturity" is that _____ _____ reflected in one's life where that person displays the combined attributes of being experienced, versed, grounded and knowledgeable in a particular way of life.

©Copyright 2008. May not be copied without permission from the publisher. All rights reserved.

Issues of Control

THIS WEEK'S FOCUS:

In order to move your child along this path from dependence to independence, you must begin a process of handing over control of your teen's life to your teen.

Homework Day One

Who Is In Control?

If you ask yourself who is in control in your family, you'd probably answer, "It's me, as a parent, I am in control." That is appropriate, and has probably been a good thing up to this point. When a child is young, parents are fully in charge, and the child is fully dependent.

As a child grows into the teen years, a parent's job is to move them from the dependent state they've always known, to independence. They need to shift from having no responsibilities to taking responsibility for every area of their life and therefore shift from immaturity to maturity. By the time they leave your home, you want them capable of making wise decisions.

Look up this scripture: Proverbs 25:28 (NIV)

"Like a city whose walls are broken down is a man who lacks _____."

 On the next page, rank what represents your level of control over the following areas of your teen's life for each of the following areas, and then ask your teen to rate their level of control over the same areas of choice. Compare your answers.

If you find it difficult to "rate" your level of control, ask someone close to you to help. Then, ask your child to also "rate" how much control you exert over these areas of his life.

This exercise is to help you see where you might need to start handing over control to your teen, or identify some areas where you need to exert a little more control, especially if you are seeing immaturity or irresponsibility in an area.

The goal is balanced control, and handing over control to your teen in a balanced manner (we'll talk more about how to do that later in this lesson.)

You	Your Child	Area of Control Over Your Teen
___	___	Dress and appearance
___	___	School choice
___	___	Time spent on homework
___	___	How they spend money
___	___	How they earn money
___	___	What subjects they study in school
___	___	Who they can spend time with
___	___	After-school activities
___	___	Music they listen to or buy
___	___	Entertainments like movies, games, or outings
___	___	Dating
___	___	How they keep their room
___	___	Cell phone and computer use

(1 = low control, 5 = high control)

 How difficult is the process for you of changing to a new level of control?

_____

_____

When it comes to handing over control to your teen, do you feel you are right on time, a bit behind, or a bit ahead of schedule according to their age and maturity? Rank yourself below.

1	2	3	4	5	6	7	8	9	10
I am a little ahead			I am right on time			I am a little behind		I am behind	

 How do you think this affects your teen?

_____

_____

 Key Thoughts

Your teen wants to be in control, and needs to learn how to be in control. That happens when a parent begins to hand over control and allow the teen to get some experience with it.

Homework Day Two

Gaining Independence

Gaining independence can be a difficult process for both you and your child. The goal is for your child to learn how to make wise decisions by the time he leaves your home. This involves more than teaching him the basics of how to handle money, how to pick the best classes for their education, or how to handle driving responsibly. It's training your child to know the difference between a wise choice and a foolish choice.

Developing wisdom comes from practice in decision-making, assessing the outcomes, and making better decisions the next time. (Remember O – R – E? Wisdom comes through a process of Observation, Reflection, and Experience!)

Look up this scripture: Hebrews 5:14 (NIV)

"But solid food is for the mature, who by _____ _____ have trained themselves to distinguish _____ from _____."

From the list of control items in Day One, choose three areas where you need to begin handing over more control, or exert a new measure of control. Write down your ideas for implementing this change with your teen:

Example: Instead of choosing all my child's clothes for school, I will give her the money I've budgeted and allow her to choose what she wants to wear. I will expect her to honor our family rules regarding modesty in her choices.

_____

_____

You must be deliberate in giving a teen the opportunity to show what they can handle by asking them to do so, even before you really believe they are ready. In fact, you should expect them to make mistakes along the way.

Don't bail them out or condemn their failures. Instead, give your teen the opportunity to think about a better way for the next time they are faced with the same decision.

You might be thinking that it would be better to wait until your child begins to show some responsibility before you begin to trust him with more. But if you wait to see your child behaving responsibly, you may never hand over control!

 Is there any area you've offered your teen more control, and had to take it back? What happened?

_____

_____

 What more can you do to positively direct your teen in an area he is seeking to control, but struggling?

_____

_____

Key Thought

A child's powers of discernment are developed through constant practice. So, give them opportunities to practice!

Homework Day Three

Two Problems: Under-Control and Over-Control

Under-Control

There are two mistakes parents make when it comes to the issue of control. The first is not setting any limits, becoming more of a peer than an authority figure in your child's life. I see this happen often in the life of a child who's parents divorce. Parents feel guilty for what they put their child through, or can't deal with their child's anger, and fail to set limits. Or, sometimes mom or dad is just a pushover.

> "Children consistently raised this way often remain selfish, demanding, independent, and aggressively controlling as adults." –Dr. Henry Cloud

It's been my experience that a child wants limits, and they want to learn to be in control of their life.

Do you see yourself as an under-controlling, or having trouble saying "no" to your child?

_____

_____

Name some areas where your child's behavior might be in response to a lack of limits in his life?

_____

_____

 Key Thought

If you don't set limits and teach a teen self-control, they will feel unprepared for life, and be frustrated and angry when faced with adulthood. They may even become rebellious in an attempt to establish independence and become more self-controlled.

Homework Day Four

Over-Control

The second mistake in parents today, even more than under-control, is over-control. Well-intentioned parents seeking to protect their child from the evils of this world will control every aspect of their child's life.

Over-control is driven by fear. Fear of letting go, or have difficulty with the fact that your child is growing up in a difficult world. Fear that the absence of self-control in your child will get him into trouble or hurt and therefore you step in and become more controlling.

While a major responsibility of good parenting is certainly to control and protect a child, parents must make room for the child to learn to take responsibility for their own choices. Often, the more immature a child appears to be, the more controlling a parent feels he should be.

Issues of control must be age-appropriate, and if your child is a pre-teen or irresponsible and immature, then you will need to remain in control over some things.

But don't shelter a child. The absence of exposure to the things of this world is no guarantee that your child will grow into an adult with godly character. Your child may do well as long as he continues to dwell in the sheltered environment of your home, but when he moves on it may undermine his ability to function in a world he's never known.

Exposure to the real world makes an opportunity for some very interesting discussions with your child, especially as they begin to wise-up after making a mistake or two.

"Over-controlled children are subject to problems of enmeshment conflicts, and may have trouble setting and keeping firm boundaries. Their creativity may be stifled and they may never take risks." –Dr. Henry Cloud

Look up this scripture: Romans 12:2 (NIV)

"Do not _____any longer to the pattern of this world, but be transformed by the _____of your mind. Then you will be able to _____and _____what God's will is—His good, pleasing and perfect will."

What does this scripture say a believer should NOT do?

_____

_____

What helps a believer become transformed into His likeness?

_____

_____

Once a believer's mind is renewed, what two ways helps him determine God's will, or know what is good, acceptable, and perfect?

_____

_____

How does this help your understanding of how to go about handing over control of more things to your child?

_____

_____

Key Thought

A parent's well-intentioned hedge of protection may actually keep a teen from gaining the discernment he needs in order to "not" be conformed to this world. And, he will miss out on the opportunity to discern what it truly means to be "in the world, but not of it."

Homework Day Five

Here are some ways to begin the process of giving your child more control:

1. Stop Lecturing, Start Discussing

When was the last time you really listened to your teen? When was the last time your teen asked you how you were doing? I tell parents all the time – take one day and just be quiet. Do nothing but listen. You may find you have a problem with listening to your teen.

2. Lead with a Question, Leave with a Question

Ask your child his opinion. Doing so imparts a sense of value to his opinion. It's a good place to start. Lead discussions with a question, and wait for his answer without giving your opinion.

3. Ask Your Child to Begin to Make More Decisions.

"Where should we go to eat tonight? What would be good for us to do on this year's vacation? What movie should we get this Friday? What charities should we support?"

4. Ask for Their Input or Viewpoint

What do you think would be the best thing to do in this situation? How would you discipline your teen differently? What you do think about a situation at school?

5. Give Them an Opportunity to Respond.

They may not respond appropriately at first, give them another opportunity to get it right.

6. Set your Boundaries and Make Them Clear.

Don't move away from your relationship with your child if they mess it up.

For example, if you see your teen watching an inappropriate movie, ask them – "Is this an appropriate movie for you to be watching?" Allow them the opportunity to respond as they should, by turning the movie off. Let them come to the decision on their own. Ask first, and give them the opportunity. If their immaturity causes them to not respond as they should, then move in and make the decision to change the channel or turn the TV off.

7. Help Your Teenager Learn How to Say "No," by Honoring it When They Do.

This doesn't mean it is okay to say "no" to your authority or your rules, but about other simpler choices they may have in their life. And reward them when you learn that they said "no" to doing wrong things with their friends or "no" to going along with the crowd. Make a big deal of it.

8. Model Humility, and Admit When You are Wrong.

9. Shift Some Control Back to Your Teen, Before You Think They Need It or Can Handle It.

10. Force Them to Take Responsibility for Their Decisions.

For example, if you give them money for gas, and they spend it on food, then they will have to figure out how to get more gas money. Don't just give them more gas money. Let them walk, if necessary.

Another example might be that you will pay for their insurance while they are in high school, but you expect them to find a job and pay for their own insurance once they are out of school. Or, if they get a speeding ticket, they can choose to attend Safe Driving School and get the ticket points removed from their record, or not attend the school and pay for their fine and their own insurance from then on.

11. Encourage Your Teen in Their Good Decisions.

Point your comments toward their successes, not their failures.

Don't say, "I told you so," or, "I should have made that decision instead of you." Instead, ask them, "What would you do if you were in my position?"

12. When Your Teen Responds with Maturity and Responsibility, then Move Them Up to the Next Level.

Expand the limit and expectations and expect them to meet new requirements.

For example: "Honey, I think it's great that you have a job now. If you are willing to save $2,500 dollars from working, I will match it and help you buy your first car."

What are the positive or negative results for the way you have handled the issue of "who is in control" in your home? What can you do to improve the way you are handling the control issue?

_____

_____

What is your motivation for allowing your child to make decisions?

_____

_____

Think of 2 or 3 questions you could begin to ask your child this week in order to start transferring control over to your child?

Example: What movie do you think would be a good choice for our family this week?

_____

_____

Name some examples of things your child is responsible for in your home? How well does your child shoulder responsibility? What new limits might you need to set into place to help your child be more responsible?

_____

_____

Outline five areas of relinquishing control you will begin to work on with your child for the next six months and share them with your classmates.

1._____

2._____

3._____

4._____

5._____

Key Thought

If you do all the thinking, and make all the decisions for your child, it may stifle their creativity. They may never take risks as adults, and they may never understand the difference between good and evil.

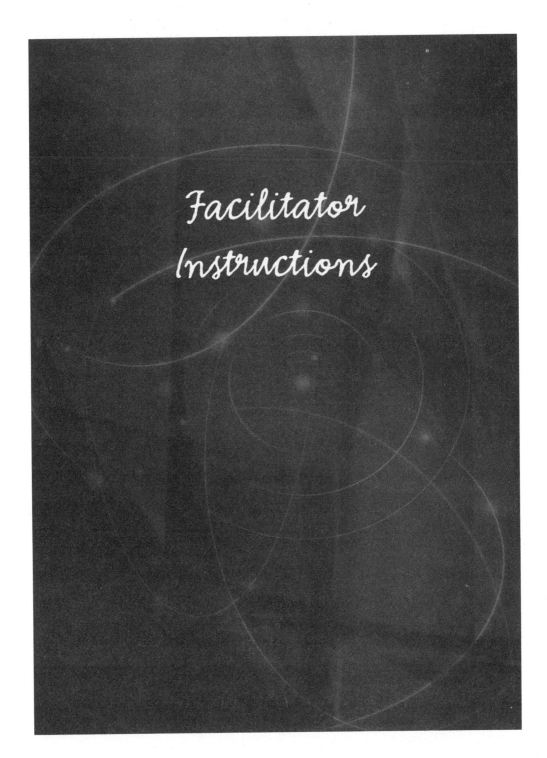

Facilitator
Instructions

Instructions for Facilitators

This is an eight-lesson study created to encourage parents in building healthy family relationships. The focus is helping parents help their child know they are not alone in their struggles.

Pastors or small group leaders can offer this training with confidence in knowing that the lessons are based on biblical principles of building godly relationships. Parents, youth workers and teachers will learn how to create an area for relationship that allows a teen to work through their difficulties with healthy boundaries, and growing maturity.

Kit Contents

* Eight Lessons (20-25 minutes each) on DVD (Set aside 9 weeks for using this series, as homework is assigned after the first video lesson, and completed the week following lesson eight.)

* Workbook with Leader Instructions.

* Promotional Materials – color posters, bulletin inserts, reminder cards, and a CD with ads and other promotional clip art.

* Audio (MP3) version of all lessons.

* Demo DVD.

Target Audience

Parents, grandparents, foster parents, youth workers, counselors, church staff, and teachers will benefit from the lessons.

Format Options

60-Minute Group Study Format

20 - 30 Minutes – Welcome

> Warm-up, introductions, and time for opening prayer.
> After the first week, review and discuss last week's homework questions before viewing next lesson.

20 - 25 Minutes – View Next Lesson

5 Minutes – Wrap up This Week's Lesson and Assign New Homework

Closing

90-Minute Group Study Format

10 - 15 Minutes – Increase your time for welcome, warm-up, introductions.
> After the first week, review and discuss last week's homework questions before viewing next lesson.

30 - 45 Minutes – Review of Last Week's Homework Questions

20 - 25 Minutes – View Next Lesson

5 - 10 Minutes — Wrap up This Week's Lesson and Assign New Homework

Closing & Prayer

Promotion and Planning

- ☐ *Meeting place assigned and posted*
- ☐ *Lights and temperature set*
- ☐ *Tables and chairs arranged*
- ☐ *Materials available*
- ☐ *Name tags, extra pens, registration forms, extra workbooks, current DVD lesson*
- ☐ *Equipment ready*
- ☐ *TV and DVD player connected and sound levels tested*
- ☐ *DVD cued*
- ☐ *Marker board or chalk board, extra marker pens or chalk*
- ☐ *Greeters to welcome participants and hand out materials*
- ☐ *Drinks or refreshments, if they are part of your plan*

Equipment Needed

For Larger Groups:
You will need a lectern, a table for materials, a TV or monitor, a DVD player, extension cords, and perhaps a marker board with pens or chalkboard and chalk

Use a large TV, if possible (27" or more) for the best impact. If your group is very large, consider using a video projection with sound system. Make sure everyone can see and the video clearly.

Room Arrangement

Whatever it takes to make sure your group is comfortable and able to take notes while viewing the lessons. Participants should be able to see one another during discussion time. Breaking into discussion groups of 10-15 is recommended for very large study groups.

Leader Guide
Discussion Group Format

Be upbeat, alert, cheerful and sensitive to every group member. Attendees may be dealing with great difficulties in their home as they seek to find help for a struggling teen. Encourage open discussion but remind the group of the confidential nature of each person's comments.

As you prepare for each session, always ask God to guide and speak through you in the power of the Holy Spirit. Your own parenting experiences may provide a meaningful backdrop for leading this study, so be willing to openly share your experience as it applies.

Welcome

First Week

Set aside 9 weeks to complete this series with your discussion group. Since there is no homework until after the first lesson, use the extra time in your first week for group members to introduce themselves and talk about their interest in attending the class. Perhaps they are facing a challenge with their teen and need more help. Perhaps they are interested in honing their parenting skills.

Also, introduce Mark Gregston to the group by reading from Mark's biographical information at the front of this workbook. Have class members write down Heartlight's web address for future reference. Also instruct the group on how the class will run, to complete the homework and come prepared for next week's discussion from homework material.

After the First Week

Open the discussion time using last week's homework assignment. Present each discussion question, reminding the group of important points when necessary. Share from your own experience or allow group members to share theirs. Ask the group to work together on answers if needed.

Introduce the new topic for the next lesson briefly by giving the title of the lesson. Begin audio or video lesson, encourage group members to follow along in their workbooks and take notes on Mark's teaching using the Lecture Notes page provided in each workbook at the beginning of a new lesson.

Watch video lesson (25-30 minutes)

Quickly review lesson. Assign homework for next week, and remind group members to prepare to share some of their answers. If you need more time on a particular area, agree to continue the discussion for another week.

Close and Dismiss

Reminder...
If anyone misses Lesson 1 or 2, they can view those online. Go to http://www.dealingwithtodaysteens.org/video.html.
(Best with a high-speed internet connection)

More Trusted Resources From
Teen Parenting Expert Mark Gregston

A broad spectrum of helps and resources are available to parents and youth workers from *Heartlight Ministries*...

Printed, Audio and Video Resources
Heartlight Resources
www.heartlightresources.com

National Radio
The Voice of Heartlight – *1-hour weekly radio program*
www.heartlightradio.org

Parenting Today's Teens – *1-minute daily radio spots*
www.parentingtodaysteens.org

Counseling and Coaching
Heartlight Residential Program for Teens
www.heartlightministries.org

Family Crisis Coaching – *coaching by phone*
www.familycrisiscoaching.com

Conferences
Dealing With Today's Teens – *small group & church conferences*
www.dealingwithtodaysteens.org

Families in Crisis Conference – *a weekend on-campus retreat*
www.familycrisisconference.com

Online Articles
Parenting Today's Teens – *blog and articles by email*
www.markgregston.com

Teen Parenting Tips – *daily teen parenting tips*
www.parentingteentips.com

Radio Programs Online
www.heartlightradioonline.com

Our Family Belief System

Every child wants structure and desires to know their boundaries. They want to take control of their lives by knowing what's required of them.

-R.H. CONNER

IMPLEMENTING CHANGE & AVOIDING CHAOS

developing a belief system for discipline

A WORKBOOK BY MARK GREGSTON

Implementing A Belief System

Change is not easy. And most of us don't like it. But without change, we are choosing to remain the same, and preventing the hand of God to further develop us, our relationships, and members of our family into the people He desires us to be.

God has called you in your role as a parent for a purpose that asks for and demands "better" for you and your family. So let me encourage you to "be the one" to stand for something good, honorable, and necessary. For without change, you all might end up in a place where you really didn't want to be. Worse yet, you might never experience what God has in store for your family by adhering to His principles.

Most times, the same old patterns of parenting that you used in the early elementary school years, continue into the adolescent years. And when they do, parents quickly learn the old ways of yester-year don't work very well with today's teens. The need for changing your parenting style becomes obvious.

Hopefully, this workbook will give you time to reflect on what you desire for your family, and come to the understanding of what God wants to do within your family as well. It is your time to make a change, to set a new path, and to establish some needed areas that have been forgotten along this sometimes struggling path called parenting.

It's also a time to stop some "stuff" that just doesn't need to happen any more. The temporary challenge of implementing change is worth the long term results of meeting greater needs within your family.

As I said, change Is tough. But hang in there, and you'll see that the efforts put into changing some "old ways" and implanting some new ways will be most beneficial for your family's future.

May God richly bless your efforts as you tackle the important task of change placed before you.

Mark Gregston

STEP ONE: Determine Your Beliefs

I believe that nothing good happens to a teen who is out of the house after midnight. You can talk until you are blue in the face to try and convince me otherwise, but I won't change my belief.

It's hard to argue with what someone truly believes, isn't it? Once you understand your beliefs, you can build rules for your home based upon those beliefs. In my case, everyone in my home abides by a curfew.

Your teen may argue against your beliefs, but it will be a fruitless exercise. **You can't argue with what someone believes.** You may believe that smoking is bad for your health, so you don't allow it in your home. Your teenager may not hold the same belief, *but it doesn't matter.* This is what YOU believe. Your teenager will decide for himself whether or not to smoke, and suffer the consequences if he chooses to do so.

You begin building your belief system for discipline by identifying what you really believe about the way your home should run. Ask yourself what is appropriate for your family. What do you believe about education, church attendance, family time, jobs, work, cleanliness, and more? Once you establish these beliefs, you can communicate them to your child.

As mentioned earlier, it's important to keep your belief system current so that it is relevant to your child at any given point in his life. For example, a four year-old child doesn't need a curfew, so don't make it part of your belief system. Pre-teen kids do need curfews, but not as late as older teens, and they may be allowed out only on non-school nights. The point is to keep your belief system appropriate to your child and their current age.

WHERE DO BELIEFS COME FROM?

Traditions. The foundation of your belief system will be you and your spouse, and it will probably be affected by the way you both were raised. Your home may or may not operate exactly the same way as your parents' home did. If you grew up in a difficult home setting, you might change many things about the way your home is run. There may also be elements in your upbringing you *will* incorporate into your home.

For example, if your parents provided a family vacation every year, and it had positive effects, then your belief system will probably include an annual family vacation as an important way for your family to spend time together.

If your parents taught you responsibility by allowing you to work for the things you wanted, you may likewise believe it's best for your children to work to earn things they want. These traditions, or generational beliefs, are ideas that are passed down from grandparent to parent to child. Consider your personal family traditions by asking the following questions: *(Feel free to jot down any notes or thoughts as you go through these sections.)*

What are your family traditions?

Which traditions are beneficial to the family? Which are not?

What do you believe about holidays?

What do you expect from your teen during family vacations?

Are non-family members allowed to come on family vacations?

How much time should your family spend together every week?

Should your teen be allowed to work while still in school?

How many hours per week should your teen work?

When is bedtime during school, weekends, holidays?

What happens when teens aren't getting enough sleep?

How often do you visit extended family?

What are some ways you parent differently than your parents?

Spiritual Beliefs. Your belief system should be closely tied to your relationship with God. The Bible is our best reference on how to live honorably and in harmony with God and man. It is an excellent resource for establishing God's ideals in your home. Your **spiritual beliefs** will address your child's character traits, spiritual training, and issues like honesty, obedience and respect.

What do you believe about family church attendance?

How often should your child should participate at church?

Can your teen choose what they'll do for spiritual training?

What is the appropriate attire for church?

Should your teen participate in mission trips?

How will you teach your child about giving to charity?

Functional Beliefs. Your functional beliefs relate to everyday living. You may believe that bedrooms need to be cleaned on a periodic basis and that each family member must perform certain chores in the home. You may believe that your attendance at your child's sports activities is a good way to encourage and support your child. **These are functional beliefs.** They address the daily habits and quirks unique to each individual in the family. When considering your functional beliefs, take into account the following topics:

Family Obligations & Requirements

Household Chores & Duties

Money & Allowances

Social Activities & Curfew

School, Homework & Grades

Volunteer & Charity Work

Extracurricular Activities & Sports

Home School, Private School

High School and College Education

Personal Cleanliness

Diet & Exercise

Medical Issues

Extended Family Relationships

Privileges. It is important that your belief system address the privileges allowed your teen. These privileges can include use of the car, cell phone, computer, tools, or electronics. You should have a plan for when these privileges will be implemented or revoked.

Can your teen stay up later than younger siblings?

When can they use the computer?

When are they allowed to drive the car?

Can they have a cell phone? A text plan?

Is your teen allowed to host a party in your home?

Can your teen use your electronic equipment (cameras/video systems)?

Social Engagements. Within your belief system, you should establish what constitutes appropriate behavior for social engagements. Consider the following questions.

When is your teen allowed to spend time with friends?

When is an adult chaperone required?

Can your teen have friends over when you are not home?

At what age will your child be allowed to date?

What is your stance on overnight outings? Extended trips?

Will your child be allowed social time on the internet?

Morals. You and your spouse will integrate your morals into your belief system. To clearly define your moral standards, ask yourself the following:

What do you believe about honesty & trustworthiness?

What about respect & obedience?

What is your stance on purity?

What about social accountability?

Who defines lawfulness?

What moral expectations do you have of your child?

Which entertainments support your moral beliefs, and which do not?

Application

Identifying your boundaries and determining your beliefs is a time-consuming process, but well worth the investment. As you consider these sources of your beliefs, write down your ten most important beliefs on the worksheets in the back cover. When you understand what you truly believe about how your home should function, you have the basis for moving toward the next step, which is to create and implement rules and consequences.

Sharing A Story

Matt was a young man that violated a rule set up for his benefit. That rule was simple: As long as he was underage, he wasn't allowed to drink alcohol. It was set up to insure that there wasn't going to be a dangerous mixture of alcohol and immaturity that could result in disaster. It was set up to insure his safety and the safety of others, and to protect him from ending up in jail for breaking the law.

But Matt broke the rule and he got drunk. He and some friends saw keys in a car and they decided to steal it. He drove the car and, like many who drink and drive, he didn't follow the speed limit. He rolled the car, and two of his friends died that night. Matt ended up in prison for nine years.

When Matt broke the rule, the effect rippled. His violation of one rule led to disregard for a number of others. Families were devastated and lives were destroyed. By breaking a rule set up protect him, Matt suffered a life-changing, eternal consequence. It changed his life and the lives of many others, and can never be erased.

STEP TWO: Develop Rules

Rules are set up to insure that people get to a place where they want to go, and to not end up in a place where they don't want to go.

Rules are intended to help the person subject to the rules. It is important for your teen to understand that rules are in place for their protection and benefit.

RULES - NOT RULING. Too often rules are established to demonstrate parental authority or control. They are displayed on the refrigerator in order to run the house. Attempts like this miss the real purpose of having rules and rebellion from your teen often ensues. Instead of establishing rules to control your child, establish rules to give your child the power to make the right decisions and gain control over his own life.

> Rules are expectations and guidelines for behavior that support your family boundaries and beliefs.

Most of us work for companies that have a policy manual. We follow the policies because they are a requirement of our employment and by following them, we receive financial benefits and privileges. The rules allow us to know what to expect, how to act, and how not to act if we want to keep our jobs. Likewise, the rules within your family belief system will help each family member know what is expected of them, how to act, where the lines are drawn between right and wrong behavior, and the consequences for stepping over the line.

174

How do you go about creating and implementing rules that will effectively guide your teen for their own good, and for the good of your entire family? Here are some guidelines:

RULE 1: RULES ARE FOR YOUR CHILD'S BENEFIT. The ultimate intent of creating and enforcing rules in your home is that of keeping a child's poor choices from consuming him, and destroying his relationships with others. Rules for your home will most likely fall into three main areas of concern, which are foundational to all other character issues. They are **honesty, obedience,** and **respect.**

RULE 2: ASK THE QUESTION. Before establishing a rule, ask yourself if the rule will help build your child's character and cause him to become more mature or responsible. Does this rule push your child toward self-control? If not, then you should rethink the rule and your motivation for making it.

RULE 3: USE COMMON SENSE. Rules need to make sense. We can all think of rules set down by our own parents that made no sense at all. Make sure your rule serves to benefit your child.

RULE 4: KEEP IT RELEVANT. Rules should be relevant, attainable and beneficial, not a source of shame, frustration, or failure. Ask yourself *"How much will this rule matter after my child is grown or I am no longer in the picture?"*

Rules need to evolve and keep in line with the growing maturity of your teenager. Out of date, irrelevant or demeaning rules will lead to animosity, loss of respect and rebellion. They can also lead to confusion about consequences, since outdated rules are often not enforced. Regularly update your rules and restate them to your teenager, awarding them with freedom and added privileges for the progress they make.

RULE 5: ENFORCE RULES WITH REASONABLE CONSEQUENCES. For teenagers, the loss of a privilege can be a powerful consequence. Sometimes they don't realize how many privileges they enjoy until they lose them for a time.

At one time years ago, we had several teenage boys living with us in our home. Based on the worsening condition of their bathroom, I could see that they needed help with exercising more self-control. So, I told them, *"Guys, from now on you need to clean your own toilet and keep your bathroom clean. If not, you could lose it."*

Unfortunately, they ignored the rule and the mess got even worse. The once pearly white toilet bowl turned horrible shades of brown.

So, one day I just took the entire toilet out! I literally removed it from the house. By that time, the toilet needed to be replaced anyway, and I thought not having it for awhile would be a good learning opportunity.

When they got home from school there was nothing but a little hole in the floor where the brown toilet used to stand, and they said, *"Where are we supposed to go?"*

I replied, *"Aim well! I'm sorry, the rule is that you need to clean your toilet and keep your bathroom clean. If you won't clean it, you can't have it."*

After a few days of not aiming too well, and the smell becoming unbearable, they came to me asking me what they needed to do to get the toilet back. I told them they could have the toilet back on the condition that they clean the bathrooms in the whole house for the next several months. They readily agreed, and we installed a new toilet. They cleaned all the bathrooms for a few months, and learned the importance of taking better care of things. **They also learned that when you break a rule, you pay the consequences.**

> Setting up rules and enforcing consequences are the best ways to help your child learn right from wrong, and to change from selfish to unselfish thinking.

RULE 6: KEEP RULES WITHIN THE CONTEXT OF YOUR RELATIONSHIP. When you put forth rules, make it clear that they are developed in the context of wanting your child to do well in life, and not a selfish way for you to feel better or be the one who is in control. Rules are not just about having your house operate well and gtting the chores done. In the toilet example I gave, I saw a major opportunity to teach these boys an important life principle, not just make that side of our house smell better.

Above all, keep in mind that your relationship with your child is more important than any rule. Don't tie rule-keeping or rule-breaking to your love for them, or your acceptance of them. Let them know that you will continue to love them, even when they break a rule. They may need to be reminded: *"There is nothing you can do to make me love you more, and nothing you can do to make me love you less."*

As you think about your beliefs and boundaries, line out the rules for your home, and begin to think about consequences. Decide things like: who pays for what, what time frame is expected for certain things like curfew and chores, what you expect from them for school and grades, work, their spiritual life, their friends. Teach them about your budget and what you can and cannot afford, and your expectations for spending. Address issues like respect, honesty and obedience with clear rules - no lying, no cheating, everyone gets respect. Talk with your teen about how the rules support your boundaries and beliefs for the way your home should run.

Application

Call a family meeting and work on the rules together. Include everyone in the decision-making. You, as parents, have the ultimate say, but don't hesitate to give up some ground in one area in order to gain ground in another. Know what you're willing to compromise before the meeting begins.

Use the family worksheets in the back cover to write down the new rules. Update the list as you have more time to consider and learn what rules are most important to your family's Belief System for Discipline.

About Rules

- ♥ Rules are established to reinforce your beliefs about the way your home should run, and define what is acceptable and what is not.

- ♥ Rules unite a family around a central set of beliefs and boundaries.

- ♥ Rules need to be relevant and current, and give your child direction.

- ♥ Rules will always be a part of life, and your child needs to know how to follow rules.

- ♥ Rules help a child know where the line is drawn between acceptable and unacceptable behavior.

- ♥ Rules should be adjusted as your child matures and shows more responsibility.

- ♥ Rules are different from boundaries. Boundaries pertain to the person; rules pertain to managing resources and the function of your home.

- ♥ Rules are about managing time, relationships, and resources.

- ♥ Rules should be enforced within the context of your relationship, and be based on a longing for your child to succeed.

A small group of Heartlight staff and residents were out in the woods having a blast by annihilating one another with paintballs. Afterward, I was surprised by a young man who refused to clean his paintball gun before putting it away. He defiantly stated he would not clean the gun, and unleashed a verbal tirade on me. I responded by saying, "Well, you played, and you know the rule: everybody cleans their own equipment after we play. And now, we have another problem. It is called disrespect. You are not allowed to be disrespectful."

Silence.

I continued, "Because you broke the gun-cleaning rule and were disrespectful too, you will have to work in the yard, and lose your privileges until you decide to clean the paintball gun."

Later that week, after many hours on work projects, he found me and said, "Hey I want you to know I am sorry about the thing with the paintball. Where's the gun?" As I set it out for him to clean, I said, "You are a good man, but you need to work through being disrespectful and acting like a four-year-old. It is killing your relationships. It's the reason you don't have friends around you. I want something better for you. This lesson is not about the stupid gun. It's about you."

But, he already knew that by then. The consequences had already helped him figure that out. I could have tried explaining it to him with words, but, the consequences spoke louder than any conversation. **"**

STEP THREE: Establish Consequences

A sensible person learns from correction. Proverbs 19:2b

The final step in creating a belief system for discipline in your home is to develop consequences that support your household rules. Communicating consequences ahead of time, and strictly enforcing them, helps a teen become more sensible, mature and responsible. Managing consequences is one of the most important parenting roles you fulfill. **When applied properly, consequences, more than anything else, teach a teen to think differently.**

DO CONSEQUENCES EVER FAIL? Consequences, when correctly applied, don't often fail. As a parent, you may fail by creating consequences that aren't helpful, or relevant to your teen's life. Or, worse, you don't enforce consequences at all. You rescue your teen before they feel the sting of their bad choice or inappropriate behavior. It's important to let consequences help your child learn to think for himself, and figure out the appropriate action to take.

GIVING & TAKING AWAY   How do you know what kind of consequence to apply? I believe it's good to give a teen something, teach them to do well with it, and take it away from them when they blow it. Start with a simple consequence, and increase the weight of the consequence for continued rule-breaking.

It helps to know you're your child values the most. Do they value time with friends, a text messaging plan, the car, cell phone, iPod, stereo? Do they value the fact that you pay for their car insurance, gas, trips, or participation in activities and events? Whatever your teen values the most is a good place to start taking things away.

Take away their most-valued possession for breaking your most valued rule. Take away the second thing they value most for the next most important rule on your list. If they value having a car the most, then a simple consequence might be: "If you aren't home by 9:30, then you can't use the car tomorrow." If they continue to miss curfew, increase the consequence and don't let them drive for quite awhile. Don't offer them rides. Let them take the big yellow school bus. Don't let them drive your car at all until the problem with curfew is solved completely. It may mean they don't get to drive for quite some time. If that happens, don't bail them out.

FOLLOWING THROUGH.   **Parents do well in telling their teens what they believe. They do well lecturing about rules and letting their teens know what is expected. What most parents don't do well is allowing the consequences of a teen's actions have their full affect to help curb or stop a child's inappropriate behavior or wrongful actions.**

You may want your child to change, but don't follow through on consequences because you're afraid your child might be inconvenienced, go through pain, or suffer a little. But remember: it's better to learn a lesson early in life while the consequences are lesser, than learning them as adults when consequences can be life-changing. To help you better understand this idea, here are some examples:

- If they flunk a class, let them meet with the teacher and figure out how to make up the credit.

- If they get a speeding ticket, let them pay for it, and the higher insurance premiums.

- If they get fired from a job, let them feel your comfort, but don't accommodate their foolish and blame-shifting conversations.

- If they get arrested, let them spend time in jail and understand what it is like to be locked up. I would much rather have a child locked up for one day at age 17, than to be locked up for years when they are 23.

- If they choose the wrong entertainment, let them sit home a few weekends.

- If they don't finish their homework, then take away a privilege.

- If they overdue their cell phone minutes, make them pay for the extra charges.

Your child will keep doing something until the pain from their actions is greater than the pleasure they receive. When you rescue them you may be getting in the way of what God really desires to teach them. Don't rescue them. Don't bail them out. Don't think you are helping by keeping them from feeling pain and hardship from their foolish actions. Let consequences have their full affect. Doing so will lead your teen **away** from the behavior that got them there in the first place.

IMPLEMENT CHANGE ONE STEP AT A TIME. It's important to implement changes to your discipline structure carefully, especially if you have never had much success with applying consequences for inappropriate behavior. Decide ahead of time what the consequences will be, and clearly communicate them to everyone in your family, not just your teen. If you haven't done such a good job of that up until now, then start by letting your teen know you've haven't done such a good job in certain areas of discipline, but you will make some changes that involves everyone soon.

> Letting your teen know what will happen in advance is a key part of the success of your belief system.

Give them time to adjust to the idea that things will be different before you let them know exactly how it will look. Then, call everyone together and work out your ideas for the new rules and consequences together.

Your teen may surprise you and come up with even stricter requirements than you originally planned. And, when it comes time to give consequences, your teen knows exactly what to expect, and exactly why to expect them.

MORE SERIOUS CONSEQUENCES. Breaking household rules is one thing. Life-changing, illegal, or dangerous behavior calls for serious consequences that get your teen's undivided attention.

A teen needs to know you will never support self-destructive, immoral or illegal behavior. The consequences for this type of problem must be drastic, and may include removing them from school, refusing to bail them out of jail when they are clearly at fault, administering drug tests as a requirement of staying in your home, participation in counseling, or taking medication as prescribed.

TOUGH & TENDER. There are two sides to administering consequences, the tough and the tender. The tough side is saying to your child, *"I will stand in front of you and stop you when you are doing something that is wrong."* The tender side is, *"I want something more for you, for your own good."* Above all, it's critical for your child to know *"Nothing you do will make me love you more; nothing you do will make me love you less."*

LIMIT THEM BUT OFFER RELATIONSHIP. Your teen needs to experience a taste of the character of God in the way you discipline and love them. They want the strength of a warrior and the tender, caring side of your help to get them through their difficulties. Make it part of your belief system to spend time together, even if your teen is suffering the consequences of a poor choice or bad behavior.

Application

Continue using the spreadsheet in the back of the book to write down consequences as they relate to what you believe should happen with discipline in your home. As you have more time to consider and learn what consequences and rewards are most important to your own family's Belief System for Discipline, take time to update them. Don't forget to consider both positive and negative consequences.

About Consequences

- ♥ Managing consequences is one of the most important parenting roles you fulfill.

- ♥ When applied properly, consequences, more than anything else in their life, teach a teen to think differently in a way that lecturing or telling them cannot.

- ♥ Consequences help them figure out the right way to respond, a better way to think, and a better way to behave.

- ♥ Communicate the consequences for rule-breaking well in advance, and make sure it's clearly understood by everyone.

- ♥ Allow your teen to make mistakes, so that the consequences can teach him a more mature response for the next time.

- ♥ Make consequences relevant to your teen's life, and the lessons he needs to learn most.

- ♥ Use the things they value the most as ammunition in your arsenal of consequences. Be generous in giving them the things they want, and serious about taking them away for behaving inappropriately.

- ♥ Engage in a continued relationship of unconditional love, even when your teen faces consequences. Require your teen to spend time with you, even if they don't want to.

- ♥ Don't bail them out of the consequences. Rescuing them once means you'll just have to rescue them again.

- ♥ Consequences help push your teen in the right direction, and effectively put an end to the parenting chaos in your home.

Example Worksheet

Use this worksheet as an example for your own worksheet on the interior of this cover.

Areas Of Change:

1. Family members will treat one another with respect at all times.

2. All family members will abide by the law, and not participate in any intoxicating substance use or abuse.

3. Family members will participate in wholesome forms of entertainment.

4. No one gets to verbally dump on anyone else.

5. We will ask permission before taking anothers things for our own use.

6. Family members will be truthful & kind

7. We will limit unhealthy or illegal influences in our home.

8. Mom and Dad will not be taken advantage of financially.

Beliefs	Rules	Consequences
We believe everyone deserves to be treated with respect.	Talk with respect to one another. Talk with respect to your parents. Talk with respect to people inside and outside our home.	Minor Infraction: loss of a minor privilege. Significant Infraction: loss of 2 minor privileges. Major Infraction: loss of major privilege
We believe drugs, smoking, and underage drinking jeopardizes the health and safety of family members.	No smoking if you are under the age of 18. No drinking if you are under the age of 21. No intoxicating substances or illegal use of any drug, no drugs in our home, no friends using drugs.	Minor Infraction: grounded one month. Significant Infraction: loss of many privileges for several months, drug counseling. Major Infraction: to be discussed (if over 18, may need to permanently leave our home).
We believe that there are certain kinds of music, television, computer games and books that can be harmful to the emotional and spiritual growth of our family.	Movies rated PG-13 and R are to be viewed only with parent approval. Games, books & tv with violence and/or sexual overtones are subject to review and approval. Music with violence, profane language, depressing and/or sexual overtones are subject to review and approval.	Minor Infraction: loss of the specific item (book, cd, etc.). Significant Infraction: loss of the privilege of that particular entertainment for one week. Major Infraction: loss of the privilege for same entertainment for one month or more.

184

Family Worksheet

Beliefs	Rules	Consequences

Beliefs	Rules	Consequences